Translated Texts for Historians

This series is designed to meet the needs  medieval history and others who wish to br source material, but whose knowledge of L to allow them to do so in the original lan Imperial and Dark Age texts are currently u... it is hoped that TTH will help to fill this gap and to complemeni ... secondary literature in English which already exists. The series relates principally to the period 300–800 AD and includes Late Imperial, Greek, Byzantine and Syriac texts as well as source books illustrating a particular period or theme. Each volume is a self-contained scholarly translation with an introductory essay on the text and its author and notes on the text indicating major problems of interpretation, including textual difficulties.

Editorial Committee

Sebastian Brock, Oriental Institute, University of Oxford
Averil Cameron, King's College, London
Henry Chadwick, Peterhouse, Cambridge
John Davies, University of Liverpool
Carlotta Dionisotti, King's College, London
Robert Markus, University of Nottingham
John Matthews, Queen's College, Oxford
Raymond Van Dam, University of Michigan
Michael Whitby, University of St Andrews
Ian Wood, University of Leeds
Jan Ziolkowski, Harvard University

General Editors

Gillian Clark, University of Liverpool
Margaret Gibson, University of Liverpool
Christa Mee, Birkenhead

Cover illustration Lid of the 'Aemiliana' sarcophagus in St Bertrand-de-Comminges.

Already published

Translated Texts for Historians
Volume 1

Second Edition

Gregory of Tours: Life of the Fathers

Translated with an introduction by
EDWARD JAMES

Liverpool
University
Press

First published 1985 by
Liverpool University Press
PO Box 147, Liverpool, L69 3BX

Second impression 1986
Second edition 1991

British Library Cataloguing-in-Publication Data
A British Library CIP Record is available
ISBN 0 85323 327 6

Printed in Great Britain at the
Alden Press in the City of Oxford

CONTENTS

PREFACE AND ACKNOWLEDGEMENTS

This is the first translation of Gregory of Tours' *Life of the Fathers* into English. The work consists of twenty short saints' lives, nearly all concerning ecclesiastics who lived in the sixth century; some were known to Gregory of Tours personally, and some were related to him. The saints in question are listed on the Contents page (where I have reproduced Gregory's own contents page, as also on p. 1: the titles given at the head of each life differ slightly). Whether by design or not, each Life illustrates a different facet of the Gallic church, and, taken together, they provide a fascinating cross-section of the church of Gregory's day. The *Life of the Fathers* forms not only an excellent introduction to the life and thought of Merovingian Gaul as a whole, but should also be of interest to anyone who wishes to understand the early church in England and Ireland: historians have become more and more aware in recent years of the influence of the church which Gregory describes on the evolution of Christianity in these islands.

My introduction is intended to supply the necessary background information, for those who may know little or nothing about Merovingian Gaul or Gregory of Tours; the notes are primarily intended to elucidate historical points, rather than linguistic ones. I have used the foot-notes in the standard Latin edition (by B. Krusch for the *Monumenta Germaniae Historica* series) as the basis for these notes; a debt which I acknowledge here rather than in the notes themselves.

Every translation is an approximation; I am most grateful to Dr Margaret Gibson and Dr Ian Wood for their efforts in making this attempt less of one than it might have been. Dr Gibson has been of great help, particularly with the translation itself, and Dr Wood has aided me considerably with the notes. I have taken the final decision in all cases, which was no doubt a mistake.

The first edition of this translation came out in 1985. I am grateful to the editorial board of "Translated Texts for Historians" for allowing me the opportunity of updating the introduction, notes and bibliography in this second edition, and of making some improvements to the translation. The technological advances of the last six years have also made this second edition look much better than the first: the move from a BBC computer plus daisy-wheel to an IBM-compatible plus laser printer is not unlike moving from quill to moveable type (or perhaps, in sixth-century terms, from papyrus to parchment). My thanks to the staff of the Computing Service at the University of York for their usual imperturbable cooperation, and my thanks also to Louise Harrison for typing the text and notes onto disk with extreme speed and accuracy.

In the first edition, I noted that, since Gregory intended his *Life of the Fathers* to be in part a celebration of the achievements of his own family,

> it would be appropriate to record here one other debt, more important than all the others, although it does not relate specifically to this book. This is my immeasurable debt to my parents, Max and Eileen James. I would like to dedicate this book to them, in the year in which the family celebrates the fiftieth anniversary of their wedding, on November 23 1984.

I should like to record that debt again, but I also have to record that, in December 1989, in his eighty-sixth year, my father died, having spent the last sad years of his life in Moseley Hall Hospital, near Birmingham. The second edition of *Life of the Fathers* is thus dedicated to the memory of my father's life, with love and gratitude.

Edward James
Centre for Medieval Studies
University of York

August 1991

INTRODUCTION

Gregory of Tours and his writings

The man we now know as Gregory was born in 538 or 539, perhaps in the Auvergne, a city-territory in the heart of Gaul whose capital was Clermont. He was a descendant of Roman senators, and a subject of the Germanic Frankish kings who had only a few years before succeeded the Roman emperors as rulers of Gaul. He was named Georgius Florentius, after his father and grandfather. Both his parents, Florentius and Armentaria, were of wealthy Gallo-Roman families with strong ecclesiastical traditions (see family tree no. 1). Florentius' brother Gallus had become bishop of Clermont in 525 (below, *VP* VI); the brothers both claimed descent from Vettius Epagatus, who had become one of the first Gallic martyrs, dying for the Christian faith at Lyons in 177. Armentaria's uncle on her father's side was Tetricus, who became bishop of Langres in the year in which Gregory of Tours was born, in succession to his father Gregorius (on whom see *VP* VII); her uncles on her mother's side were Nicetius (see *VP* VIII), who was to succeed his uncle Sacerdos as bishop of Lyons in 552, and Duke Gundulf, while they in turn were the sons of Florentinus, who had been offered the bishopric of Geneva in 513 (*VP* VIII 1). The children of Florentius and Armentaria continued the family traditions. One, our own author, became bishop of Tours; another married and bore a child who became prioress of the Poitiers nunnery; and a third, Peter, would surely have risen in the ranks of the clergy had he not been murdered while still a deacon in Langres (*LH* V 5).

Georgius Florentius took the name by which he is always known, Gregory (from his mother's great-uncle, the miracle-working Gregory of Langres), probably on the occasion of joining the clergy. That destiny may have been decided for him at an early age by his family (although in *VP* II 2 he presents it as the fulfilment of a personal vow). As a boy he spent some time with his great-uncle Nicetius, before Nicetius became bishop of Lyons; then he studied under Archdeacon Avitus at Clermont, before Avitus became bishop of Clermont. For a while, some time after 552, he was at Lyons with Bishop Nicetius (*VP* VIII 4); he had already become a deacon by the time he travelled to

Tours as a pilgrim to St Martin's shrine in 565 (*VSM* I 32). It has been suggested that he may have served for a time as a priest at the shrine of St Julian at Brioude in the Auvergne, which was much frequented by his family, as his own later *Miracles of St Julian* show. Then in 573 he was chosen to succeed his mother's cousin Eufronius as bishop of the see of Tours, all of whose bishops except five, he tells us with pride, had been members of his family (*LH* V 49).[1] The poet Venantius Fortunatus celebrated his arrival (*Carmen* V 3): "His merits have brought him to this honour, and his very name has destined him to be a pastor of a flock [*pastor gregis*]. Julian has sent his own pupil to Martin, and offers to his brother him whom he held dear."

Gregory was ordained bishop by Aegidius of Rheims (who appears later in Gregory's *History* as a conspirator and traitor), at the court of Sigibert, one of the three brothers who then ruled Gaul between them: Sigibert's portion included both Clermont and Tours. Only two years later, in 575, Sigibert was assassinated, and Tours fell into the hands of Sigibert's brother (and possibly assassin) Chilperic. Gregory's political position was not an easy one. Tours was not only a strategically important territory in dispute between two kings, but it was also the site of the shrine of St Martin, where sanctuary was sought by great men of the kingdom as well as petty criminals. One of the former was Chilperic's own son Merovech (*LH* V 14), who incurred the king's wrath by marrying Sigibert's widow Brunhild in an apparent attempt to secure an independent political position. Gregory was alone among the bishops at the Council of Paris in 577 in defending Bishop Praetextatus, who had married Merovech and Brunhild (*LH* V 18), and when he returned to his see he found that Leudast, the count of Tours, had conspired with a number of clerics to depose him (*LH* V 49). He weathered this storm, even though it involved him appearing in front of Chilperic in 580 to answer the charges of his enemies in Tours that he had slandered Chilperic's queen Fredegund. He was reconciled with Chilperic, or, perhaps, was forced into obedience, for we see him refusing to admit Count Leudast to communion, despite the appeal of a number of bishops, because Queen Fredegund did not wish it (*LH* V 32).

---

1. On this claim, see Piétri 1983 and Mathisen 1984.

The worst of Gregory's political problems seem to have come to an end in 584, however, when Chilperic was assassinated. The king's only surviving brother, Guntram, restored Tours to the young heir of Sigibert, Childebert II. Gregory shows himself on good terms with Guntram, whom he visited while on a state visit to Orleans, and whose dinner conversation he records (*LH* VIII 4-5). Guntram sent him on an embassy to Childebert in Coblenz in that same year, 585. In 588 Childebert sent Gregory to Guntram at Chalon-sur-Saône, to confirm the terms of a treaty established between the two kings at Andelot the previous year. It was perhaps in recognition of these services that Childebert was willing to give in to Gregory's demand in 589 that the city of Tours be exempt from taxation (*LH* IX 30), a feat celebrated in verse by Venantius Fortunatus (*Carm.* X 11). He was at Childebert's court again in 591 (*VSM* IV 26); at this period he was also much involved in settling the dispute that had arisen at the nunnery of the Holy Cross in Poitiers (*LH* IX 39-43, X 15-17 and 20). He was bishop of Tours for some twenty-one years, and it was in the midst of all his episcopal cares and duties that he wrote the various works by which he is known today. He finished his *Miracles of St Martin* in the summer of 593; he seems to have finished touching up the *History* in the following year, and he died, according to tradition, on a November 17 some time after that, perhaps in 595 but more likely in 594.

At the end of the *History* (*LH* X 31) he listed the deeds of the previous eighteen bishops. He wrote of his own achievements as nineteenth bishop, listing his building works and acquisition of relics, and ending with his literary works: (*Hist. of Franks*)

> I have written ten books of Histories, seven books of Miracles, and one on the life of the Fathers; I have commented on the Psalms, in one book; I have also written a book on the times of ecclesiastical offices.

Elsewhere he had included the *Life of the Fathers* as one of his *eight* books of miracles, and described their contents thus:

> In a first book [*GM*] I therefore included some of the miracles of the Lord, the Holy Apostles, and the other martyrs. These miracles had been unknown until now, [but] God deigned to increase them daily to strengthen the faith of believers. For it was surely improper that they disappear from memory. In a second book [*VJ*] I wrote about the miracles of Julian. I wrote four books [*VSM* 1-4] about the

miracles of St Martin, and a seventh [*VP*] about the life of
some blessed [saints] (*de quorundam feliciosorum vita*). I
am writing this eighth book about the miracles of the
confessors. (*GC*, Preface; transl. Van Dam p. 17).

The eight "Books of Miracles" are generally known as follows (with the
abbreviations I intend to use throughout):

I.   *Liber in Gloria Martyrum*: The Glory of the Martyrs. *GM*
II.   *Liber de Passione et Virtutibus Sancti Iuliani Martyris*: The
             Passion and Miracles of St Julian. *VSJ*
III-VI.   *Libri I-IV de Virtutibus Sancti Martini Episcopi*: The
             Miracles of St Martin. *VSM* I-IV
VII.   *Liber Vitae Patrum*: The Life of the Fathers. *VP*
VIII.   *Liber in Gloria Confessorum*: The Glory of the
             Confessors. *GC*[2]

Gregory clearly worked on most of his books simultaneously
during his episcopate, bringing them up-to-date, incorporating cross-
references and so on. Krusch argued from these cross-references that
VSM I was written around 581, *VSM* II by c. 587, *VSJ* at some date
between those two, and so on. *VP* does not refer to *GC* except in the
Preface; *GC* makes references to *VP* whenever it treats of the same
saints (Venantius in *GC* 15, Monegundis in *GC* 24, Senoch in *GC* 25,
Brachio in *GC* 38 and Nicetius of Trier in *GC* 92). The Preface to *GC*
quoted above also suggests that this, the last of the eight books, was put
into its final form after the others. Parts of *VP* were probably written in
the 580s (XII, XV , XVI and XIX were from before 587 according to
Krusch), but *VP* VIII and XX must have been written in 591 or 592,
and so the whole book could not have been assembled until 592 or even
later. But precise dating of any part of Gregory's works is hardly
possible; as Raymond Van Dam notes in his discussion of the dating of
GM, "Gregory was constantly revising his writings over the years."[3]

---

2. *GC* and *GM* have been translated in this series, by Raymond Van Dam; *VSM* I has
been translated in E. Peters, ed. 1975 (see below p. 132). Professor Van Dam is currently
working on *VSM* I-IV and *VSJ*, which will bring all of Gregory's miracle stories into
English translation.

3. R. Van Dam, *Gregory of Tours: Glory of the Martyrs* (Liverpool, 1988), p. 4.

The *Life of the Fathers*

Gregory of Tours is familiar to medievalists, students and teachers alike, above all for his *Decem Libri Historiarum* (*LH*), known misleadingly since the eighth century as the *History of the Franks*.[4] Yet his hagiographical works are also uniquely interesting, and the *Liber Vitae Patrum* probably most of all. There are a number of reasons why it is desirable to make it available to a wider audience in the English-speaking world. First of all, it is, for the beginner, much less confusing as an introduction to sixth-century Gaul than *LH*; it tells coherent stories, without the plethora of confusing names and the cascade of events without apparent interconnection or purpose which are, for most readers of *LH*, the first off-putting impressions. Secondly, it provides a much clearer picture than *LH* of the kind of people who made up the sixth-century Gallic church, their upbringing, training and clerical careers. It also offers an unparalleled insight into those clerical and Christian virtues Gregory himself regarded as worthy of emulation, and as such gives us some idea of the aims and appeal of the Gallic church. The lives of ordinary people in Merovingian Gaul, which seldom come before the eyes of Gregory the historian, are much more visible in the works of Gregory the hagiographer, such as *VP*. And finally, and not least important, *VP* includes essential information about Gregory's own family and background, and about his own episcopal career, all of which help us understand the author of one of the most important of all medieval histories.

The "Life of Certain Blessed Men" (as *VP* was called in *GC*, Preface), the "Life of the Saints" (in *VP*, Preface), or the "Life of the Fathers" (also in *VP*, preface), is, as its author recognised in *LH* X 31, not like the other seven books of miracles. It is not dedicated to the

---

4. Once the seventh-century editor had removed many of the chapters of *LH* referring to saints and ecclesiastical matters, then the book did indeed look rather more like a "History of the Franks". The seventh-century excisions are marked by asterisks in Lewis Thorpe's translation of the work; he, however, thought that these chapters were the additions made by Gregory in a second and/or final draft. Goffart shows conclusively that Gregory always intended his *History* to be a blend of secular and ecclesiastical history (1988, pp. 121-127), and argues forcibly not only against calling it the *History of the Franks* but also against such alternatives as *Decem Libri Historiarum*: "He called his work *Historiae*, "Histories", and presumably wished it to bear this name" (p. 120).

miracles of one saint, as *VSJ* and *VSM* were; it is not an assemblage of miracle stories about large numbers of saints, like *GM* and *GC*. Instead *VP* is a collection of twenty saints' lives, of varying lengths, all being the lives of Gallic saints and all of them (except those dealt with in *VP* I and X) connected in some way either with Gregory's own family or with the two dioceses in which he spent most of his life, Clermont and Tours. *VP* is thus a celebration of the saints of his own family (*VP* VI concerns his father's brother, *VP* VII his mother's great-uncle and *VP* VIII her uncle); it is a celebration of those saints whose miraculous powers had aided his family (*VP* II relates how St Illidius saved Gregory's life; *VP* VII tells how St Gregory of Langres cured Gregory's mother of fever; *VP* XIV tells how St Martius cured Gregory's father of fever); and it is a glorification of the two cities or dioceses most closely associated with his family and its secular and ecclesiastical power.

But Gregory undoubtedly had other aims in mind. In particular he wished, as most hagiographers did, "to encourage the minds of listeners to follow their example" (*VP*, Preface). The grammatical discussion in his Preface concerning whether the word *vita* had a plural or not obscures the issue. His use of the singular, "Life", rather than "Lives", is much more to do with his wish to point out that those who were deemed holy by God all lived the same kind of life, the life of a true Christian — all saints have the one life in Christ; a later hagiographer, Agnellus of Ravenna, disarmingly used this argument to excuse his fabrication of lives of former archbishops of Ravenna about whom he had no information at all.[5] That is not to say that Gregory does not distinguish between his saints. Most of the saints he chooses illustrate a particular aspect of the holy life, and make their own theological or moral point, which is often indicated clearly in the preface to each Life. Thus *VP* I talks of determination, *VP* VI of contempt for worldly things, *VP* VIII of predestination, *VP* X of God's help, *VP* XII of discipline, and so on. We can also get some idea of those qualities which Gregory particularly admired in his saints, or of the qualities appropriate for those who chose different paths to salvation. Gregory does not show a particular preference for either the active or

---

5. See Jones 1947, p. 63.

the contemplative life: he shows how bishops, abbots, and hermits or recluses each had a role within the church, and each had chosen a legitimate way to follow the Christian life. But his personal preferences perhaps emerge when we look at the ecclesiastics actually involved. The bishops, six of the twenty saints in *VP*, were in three if not four cases related to Gregory himself, and their aristocratic connections were emphasised. The burdens of episcopal office were considerable, as Nicetius of Trier recognised (*VP* XVII 1), but Gregory's bishops nevertheless emerge with flying colours. His abbots and hermits are not always so fortunate: they are perhaps usually of a lower social status (particularly noted in *VP* IX 1 and *VP* XX 1), they lose heart (*VP* I 1 and *VP* IX 2), they fail to make a success of communal living (*VP* IX 1), and they succumb to vainglory (*VP* X 2; *VP* XI 2), or to quarrelling (*VP* XX 3). Two of them, Senoch and Leobardus (*VP* XV and XX), have to be recalled to the paths of righteousness by their bishop, Gregory of Tours himself, in passages whose lesson is less that of the glory of the eremitical life than of the necessity to obey bishops. Gregory was as well aware as his near-contemporary St Benedict of Nursia of the perils of the solitary life, and it was perilous not only for the soul of the hermit himself, but also for episcopal authority. The fate of every successful hermit was to attract a crowd of devotees around him, which, if he lived far from the urban episcopal centre, could be a problem, providing a rival spiritual attraction and also creating a potential breeding-ground for heresy. The story of the ascetic Wulfoliac (who sat on his column near Trier, in the manner of a Syrian holy man but without the benefit of mild Syrian winters) was inserted by Gregory in the "Histories" (*LH* VIII 15-16), and was designed specifically to show how ascetics must obey their bishops. Gregory does not disapprove of extreme forms of asceticism as such, but there is a world of difference between braving frost-bite on top of a column, like Wulfoliac, and wearing a heavy stone around one's neck (and placing thorns under one's chin so as not to fall asleep) in the privacy of one's cell, as Lupicinus did (*VP* XIII 1). Private asceticism, which attracts neither crowds nor vainglory, is perfectly acceptable. Gregory's attitude is summed up in *VP* in the charming story of how Gregory of Langres used to conceal that he was living on barley-bread and water by hiding his small barley loaves among the wheaten ones, and drinking water out of an opaque cup so that people would think it was wine (VII 2).

The question of the making of an early medieval saint is confused by the problems of the translator. I have translated the word *sanctus* quite inconsistently, sometimes as "holy man" or "the holy X" and sometimes as "saint". The former would be more correct, even though the frequency of the connection between the word *sanctus* and a personal name shows that it has something of the feel of a title. Saints were not, of course, distinguished from the rest of humanity as neatly in the sixth century as they were to be after the establishment of a canonisation procedure in the twelfth and thirteenth centuries. But those who led particularly holy lives, such as all those who are dealt with in *VP*, might be marked out by God from the rest of humanity by the working of miracles. They work them during their lives, particularly miracles of healing. But, as Gregory points out, those are not certain proofs of God's favour: "The *virtus* which comes from the tomb is much more worthy of praise than those things which a living person can work in this world, because the latter can be blemished by the continual difficulties of worldly occupations, while the former are certainly free from all blemish" (*VP* II 2). Presumably Gregory has in mind that these miracles are being worked through a living man who is subject, as all living men are, to temptation and to sin; but he may also be referring to the possibility that, while alive, the holy man may be working miracles for the wrong reason, like Secundellus, whom the Devil persuades to go out and work miracles, in order that he might be tempted by vainglory (*VP* X 2). "One should weigh well what the Lord says in the Gospel: Many will say to me in that day, Lord, Lord, have we not prophesied in thy name?... and then will I profess unto them, I never knew you" (*VP* II 2). But a miracle produced by prayer to a dead holy man, or contact with the holy tomb or relics from it, is a proof that that holy man has been raised to heavens on his death by God: those miracles have been rendered beyond reproach by the holy man's death. And they are miracles which not only display God's power, but also prove that the saint has been taken to heaven, and from there looks after those who are faithful to his name. As Aigrain notes, Gregory in this text is very careful to "prove" the sanctity of each of his heroes by mentioning the whereabouts of their tombs, the frequency of miracles done there, and the churches which have been established holding their relics.[6]

A saint is revealed by miracles, therefore. But here too we have problems of translation, with one of the more ambiguous words used in late antique texts, *virtus* — as problematical in its way as *virtù* in Renaissance Italian. In the first passage I quoted in the previous paragraph I did not translate it, although at *VP* II 2 below I translate it as "virtue". It could just as well have been rendered as "power" or "miracle". (Other early medieval meanings instanced by Niermeyer include "relic", "church considered as property", "violence", "right", "force of law", "armed forces". In the plural form *virtutes* it can refer to "the powers", a rank in the angelic host.[7]) For the Christian writer it is "power" above all in the sense of "power to work miracles", and that is how it came to mean "miracle" itself, as in the title of five of Gregory's "books of miracles", VSJ and VSM I-IV. It is these miracles, of course, which so long proved a stumbling block to historians, who saw in Gregory no more than an uncritical compiler of childish and superstitious stories. We are now (thanks to the work of scholars such as Graus, and, in the English-speaking world, Peter Brown, Clare Stancliffe, Ray Van Dam[8] and, most recently, Valerie Flint and William D. McCready) better able to understand the mental world of men like Gregory, and to appreciate the literature of saints for the unique literature which it was: "Where can we turn other than to the hagio-graphic works of Gregory of Tours to learn the truly important facts about Merovingian Gaul: the dimensions of Lac Leman and the superior quality of its trout; the temptations of *civet de lapin* in the Lenten season; the first mention of the *omelette à la provençale*? The very 'concrete and fastidious' nature of this genre upsets the critics and delights the social historian in search of fragments of 'local colour'; it betrays the urgency with which men like... Gregory sought to trace the joining of past and future in their own time. For, as Gregory often says, if healing and mercy did not happen in his own days, who would

---

6. Aigrain 1953, p. 175.

7. As pointed out by Stancliffe 1983, p. 222.

8. Van Dam 1985 section IV, "The Cult of Relics in Sixth-Century Merovingian Gaul", is an excellent introduction to the cultural phenomenon for which *VP* itself is a major source.

believe that they had ever happened or ever would happen again?"[9]

The "concrete and fastidious" nature of the genre, and its vividness and colour, are admirably conveyed in Gregory's prose, although this too has only been recognised recently. The deficiencies of Gregory's Latin from the point of view of classical conventions were obvious enough, and have been ably detailed by Max Bonnet (see Bibliography). Gregory might well have agreed with Bonnet's strictures himself. There are in fact several occasions when Gregory bemoans his shortcomings as an author of Latin prose, but the Preface to *GC* offers us the most extensive self-criticism:

> I fear that when I begin to write, since I am without learning in rhetoric and the art of grammar, the learned will say to me "Uncouth and ignorant man, what makes you think that this gives you a place among writers? How do you suppose critics will receive this work, which is neither provided with artistic skill nor helped out by any knowledge of letters? You who have no useful foundation in letters, who do not know how to distinguish between nouns, who often put feminines for masculines, neuters for feminines, and masculines for neuters; who often, furthermore, do not even put prepositions in the place where the authority of the more celebrated mentors has decreed that they belong..."
> Yet I shall reply to them, saying "I do the same work as you, and by my very roughness will provide matter for your skill. For, as I think, these writings will bring you one benefit, namely, that what we describe rudely and abruptly in our turgid style you may enlarge in verse..."[10]

Gregory's mother had, as Gregory portrays it, more sense than he himself: in a vision she replied to his worries by saying "Can't you understand that we prefer the way you speak because people understand it?" (*VSM* Preface) And indeed it is generally agreed that Gregory's style is much closer to the speech of ordinary people than almost any other writer of the time. He did not reproduce the sound of that language, nor did he abandon entirely the use of "literary" words, but, as Auerbach said, "many turns, many word meanings, much of the rhythm, especially in the frequent direct discourse, were unquestionably

9. Brown 1981, pp. 81-82, referring in the last sentence to *VSM* I Preface and *GC* 6.

10. Translation by Auerbach 1965, p. 104.

taken over directly from the language that he heard around him and he himself spoke every day of his life."[11] That only appears an exceptional and refreshing achievement to anyone who has had to plough through the verbose and obscure circumlocutions of "correct" literary Latin of the fourth or fifth centuries, which must have been quite divorced from ordinary speech, and indeed almost certainly not comprehensible to most people in Gaul. The result was a Latin all his own, "a literary language with which the colloquial tongue had been fused",[12] ideally suited to the vivid description of historical events. We may doubt whether Gregory's profession of inadequacy was any more than literary convention, or a means of covering himself against criticism from the handful of Latin stylists of the old school in late sixth-century Gaul, like the Italian-born bishop of Poitiers, Venantius Fortunatus; Gregory must have been aware that his stylistic innovations were a major achievement. Thanks to the regrettable classical revival of the Carolingian Renaissance, and the resultant split of the literary and spoken languages,[13] this liveliness and immediacy were not to surface again in historical prose until the vernacular historians of the fifteenth century.

Gregory's World

To understand *VP* properly it is necessary to know something about the world in which Gregory worked and wrote. It was one that had seen "the decline and fall of the Roman Empire in the West", but we may doubt whether he viewed it in quite the same light as many modern historians. In the first two decades of the fifth century the Roman inhabitants of Gaul, like those of Britain, had lived through a series of crises that must have led many to believe that the Roman Empire, and hence the very structure of their world, was collapsing around them. There had been usurpations, peasant rebellions, and barbarian raids and invasions by sea and land, each of them threatening

---

11. Auerbach 1965, p. 109.

12. Auerbach 1965, p. 111.

13. On which see R. Wright, *Late Latin and Early Romance in Spain and Carolingian France* (Liverpool, 1982).

the stability of the Roman provinces of Gaul and the welfare of Gallo-Romans. The Rhine frontier had been definitively breached in 407, and the administration of Gaul had had to remove to the relative safety of Arles; various barbarian peoples had made permanent settlements in Gaul. But an observer at the end of the fifth century might have felt content that most of Gaul had weathered these crises remarkably well, particularly in comparison with the neighbouring province across the Channel. The establishment of friendly barbarian peoples as military protectors in the south — Visigoths in the south-west and Burgundians in the south-east — and the accommodations reached with the newcomers in the north — Romano-British refugees in the north-west and Franks in the north-east — enabled the propertied and powerful men in Gaul (like those in Gregory's own connection) to preserve much of their wealth and social influence, and possible to increase their political power. The administrative and economic structure of Gaul remained much as it had been, and, except on the eastern frontiers of the province, the newcomers adopted the Latin language of the Gallo-Romans and, fairly rapidly, their Christian religion as well. The permanent presence of an acknowledged ruler in Gaul (rather than the occasional appearance of a dubiously legitimate emperor), and a ruler who, though barbarian, was keen to imitate Roman ways with the help of Roman advisers, could be viewed by many as a distinct benefit. By the time Gregory of Tours was born, the situation was even more favourable: the Franks had largely eliminated the power of other Germanic peoples within Gaul, and kings of the Merovingian dynasty, that was to provide a kind of political stability for another two centuries, divided Gaul among themselves. To characterise this process (and the entire "fall of the Roman Empire") as "an imaginative experiment that got a little out of hand"[14] is helpful, but only if we are very clear what we mean by "a little out of hand", and from whose point of view we are making that judgement. Now that (some) historians are prepared to jettison the stated or unstated assumption of the last millennium and a half that the collapse of the Roman Empire in the West was a Bad Thing, we are better able to understand the process in an unprejudiced way. But a study of the attitude of the inhabitants of the barbarian

---

14. Goffart 1980, p. 35.

kingdoms to the departed Empire has yet to be written.

Undoubtedly the attitude of Gregory of Tours himself would play a major role in such a study. Gregory did in some ways lament the present, and feel that his world was in decline, but so did most writers in the ancient and medieval worlds. In the Preface to Book I of his *Decem Libri Historiarum* he bore in mind "those who are losing hope as they see the end of the world approaching" (no more than a familiar cliché, perhaps) and he believed that "the knowledge of literature is declining or even disappearing altogether from the towns of Gaul" (*LH*, Preface). Nevertheless, Gregory has no nostalgia for the "good old days" of the Roman Empire in the West. Roman emperors are much more likely to appear in his writings as persecutors, and the only two deeds he records of the first Christian emperor, Constantine the Great, were the poisoning of his son and the murder of his wife in a hot bath (*LH* I 36). By Gregory's day there were no more persecutions in Gaul, and the Franks were prepared to support the Catholic establishment against possible threats from heresies such as Arianism. The Church was becoming ever more wealthy and influential. "Our treasury is bankrupt", King Chilperic used to complain, "and all our wealth has been transferred to the Church. Only bishops have any power" (*LH* VI 46). Although the Frankish kings of the Merovingian dynasty did war amongst themselves, despite Gregory's appeals, they were largely successful in preventing further barbarian incursions into Gaul; they did much to pay for their own extravagances through successful campaigns outside Gaul; and they allowed aristocrats in most of Gaul to run their own localities with very little disturbance. (This last was the culmination of developments already apparent within the Empire, and no doubt welcome to the aristocrats themselves, although perhaps not to others). These and other changes, which must have been much less obvious to those who lived through them than they are to present-day historians, can all be viewed from more than one angle. The increasing difficulty the Frankish kings had in extracting taxation from their subjects, for instance, was a "decline" from Roman standards, but was welcomed by many, including Gregory of Tours himself. The closing of the public schools and the subsequent decline (though by no means extinction) of lay literacy had the effect of giving the church a much greater role in education and learning. And so on.

The Frankish kings of whom Gregory wrote were not unworthy

successors of the Roman emperors. Most of them were energetic warriors, as most successful emperors had been. Like emperors, few of them cared much for book learning, nor were they more than conventionally pious. (King Chilperic, who wrote Latin verse and took theology very seriously, earned nothing but scorn from Gregory of Tours: see *LH* VI 46). The relatively small areas over which each of them ruled allowed them to offer their subjects rather easier access than emperors had been able or willing to offer; like them they must have spent much time in dealing with petitions and legal proceedings. And, like emperors, they attracted to themselves much lurid gossip and scandal, although Gregory is restrained in what he records in comparison with his contemporary, the Greek historian Procopius, who covers the imperial couple Justinian and Theodora with an inordinate amount of traditional rhetorical abuse in his scurrilous *Secret History*. Gregory's kings are much more believable than Procopius's, above all in the vivid portrayals of three of the four sons of Chlothar I (d. 561): Sigibert (d. 575), Chilperic I (d. 584) and Guntram (d. 592).

Gregory of Tours himself, of course, is our main historical source for the world in which he was born. His writings, above all the *Decem Libri Historiarum*, dominate our understanding of sixth-century Gaul just as effectively as Bede's *Historia Ecclesiastica Gentis Anglorum* has dominated those who have tried to understand early Anglo-Saxon England. There was much that Gregory did not understand about Frankish society and kingship; Gregory's geographical horizons, even within Gaul, were limited; the range of subjects which he considered it his task to record was equally limited (although much less so than it was for Bede); his willingness to record unsubstantiated gossip, on the other hand, seems almost unlimited. Bede's monastic reticence and caution contrasts strongly with the verve (or horror) with which Gregory details the violent deeds of laymen and the peccadilloes of clerics: in the process he almost certainly gives us an unduly colourful view of early Frankish Gaul.

Bede tells us no more than what he wants to tell us; for a long time it has been assumed that Gregory is more artless, and hence a better informant. It is hard, any longer, to sustain this notion: Gregory was an able writer and intelligent man, who had a particular agenda in mind with both his historical and hagiographical writings. Goffart has recently argued forcibly for the artistic unity and complexity of

Gregory's writing.

> [The] transposition of the golden age of the Church to the
> everyday of Merovingian Gaul is the foundation of confid-
> ence that sustains the pessimism, outrage, and irreverence
> of Gregory's *Histories*.[15]

In his miracle stories Gregory celebrated the work of God and his Saints
on earth; in his *Histories*, Goffart argues, he took his cue from satire.

> Gregory's concept of the past... strikes an unexpectedly
> original note. Its irony foreshadows the Voltairian idea that
> history depicts only crimes and calamities, but Gregory, not
> stopping there, found room for the countervailing *virtutes
> sanctorum*: the mad world castigated by the holy prophet
> also contained its critic and what he stood for.[16]

The more conscious an artist Gregory appears to be, of course, the more
difficult it is today to write a history of sixth-century Gaul from his
works. We have to understand his intellectual and literary concerns, and
his personality, before we can "use" him as an historical "source"; it
may be that this translation, which introduces the more contemplative
and idealistic side of Gregory, will enable those who only know
Gregory through the *History* to get closer to an overall view of the man.

The manuscripts

Krusch lists those manuscripts in which *VP* occurs in his
edition, pp. 12-25. The most important are five (I cite his numbers): 1a
(Paris BN Lat. 2204), a ninth-century manuscript containing all
Gregory's hagiographical works, together with the *Life of St Martin* by
Sulpicius Severus; 1b (Paris BM, nouv. acq. lat., 1493) of the late ninth
or early tenth century, formerly in the library of Cluny, very similar to
1a but containing only *GM*, *VP* and *GC*; 2 (Paris BN Lat. 2205), of the
tenth century, with a carelessly written text; 3 (Clermont-Ferrand Bibl.
Mun. 11), a finely written and decorated MS of the tenth century,
lacking *VP* XVIII-XX and parts of other books; and 4 (Brussels, Bibl.
Roy., 7666-71), again of the tenth century, and containing only *VP* and
GC. These five manuscripts are all very similar — all have the same

---

15. Goffart 1988, p. 228.

16. Goffart 1988, p. 229.

gap in *VP* VIII 3, which shows they have the same ultimate source —
although no. 4 has a number of unique features: it is, for instance, the
only one to have a complete text of *VP* II 4. There are also grammatical
and orthographic features which distinguish no. 4 from the other four
manuscripts. For instance, in his *History* Gregory uses two forms of
"altar" without distinction — *altare* and *altarium*. But MSS 1a, 1b, 2
and 3 are nearly consistent in using the former, while MS 4 almost
invariably uses the latter. In some ways 4 is more carefully written. In
the quotation from Prudentius in the Preface to *VP* VI, for instance, 4
has, correctly, *parto fit*, while 1, 2 and 3 have *parturit*. So 4 is using a
different, and more accurate, source MS than 1, 2 and 3. But it also
shares some errors with 2 (*Amandi* instead of *Amanti* in *VP* IV 1,
creatus instead of *formatus* in *VP* III, Preface etc), so the scribe must
have had access also to an MS resembling 2. On the other hand,
sometimes all five MSS have the same error, as in *VP* VIII 8, where
Phronimius is put in the nominative instead of the genitive, making it
the name of the servant rather than the name of the bishop whose
servant he was. For such reasons Krusch schematised the relationship
between these manuscripts, and four hypothesised lost manuscripts, as
follows:

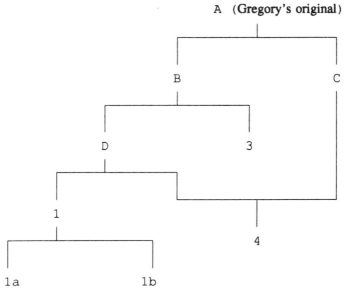

The translation

I have tried to make the translation give as much of the flavour of the original as possible. Thus, echoes of the Bible are given in "Biblical English" (actual quotations from the Bible are from the Authorised version, sometimes slightly altered). I have tried to reflect in my English the rhetorical style of the prefaces to each life, with their longer sentences and more complex structures, and to contrast them with the more direct, less "literary" style of the actual lives. Occasionally Gregory changes the tense in the middle of a passage from past to present, in order, presumably, to make the action more immediate to his readers or hearers; this too I have translated literally, although it may sound odd in English. Some of the uncertainties and problems of translation I have referred to in the notes, or in my introduction above, but there are too many such cases to discuss each individually; I simply remind readers that every translation involves guesswork. Wherever possible I have translated place-names into the modern French, German or Swiss equivalents, although I have used English equivalents where appropriate (e.g. Rheims and Cologne). I have adhered to Clermont rather than Clermont-Ferrand, on the grounds that modern inhabitants still refer to the old city in that way, rather than using the new-fangled term (which only dates back to the administrative merger with neighbouring Montferrand in 1630).

Family Tree No. 1: The family of Gregory of Tours

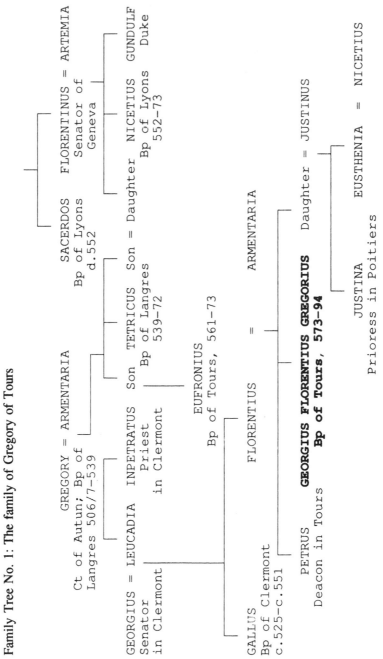

Family Tree No 2: The 6th Century Merovingian Kings

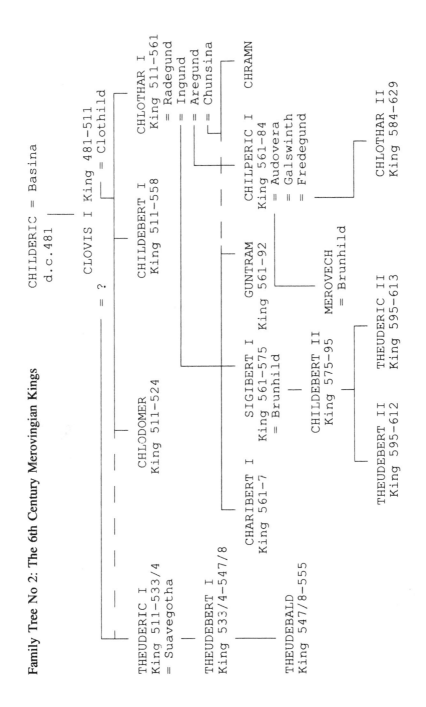

Map 1. Gaul in Gregory's day, with places mentioned in *VP*

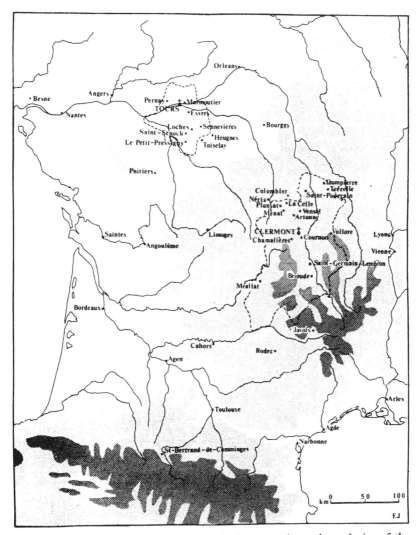

Map 2. Aquitane in Gregory's day, with the approximate boundaries of the dioceses of Clermont (the Auvergne) and Tours

TRANSLATION

HERE BEGINS THE BOOK OF
THE LIFE OF THE FATHERS,
THE WORK OF GEORGIUS FLORENTIUS
GREGORIUS OF TOURS

I had decided to write only about what has been achieved with divine help at the tombs of the blessed martyrs and confessors. But I have recently discovered information about those who have been raised to heaven by the merit of their blessed conduct here below, and I thought that their way of life, which is known to us through reliable sources, could strengthen the Church. Since the occasion presented itself, therefore, I did not want to postpone the relation of some of these things, because the life of the saints not only makes their aims clear, but also encourages the minds of listeners to follow their example.

Some people have asked us whether we should say the *vita* [life] or *vitae* [lives] of the saints. A. Gellius and several other philosophers have said *vitae*.[1] But the writer Pliny in the third book of the *Art of Grammar* says "The ancients have said 'the lives' of each of us; but grammarians did not believe that the word *vita* has a plural".[2] From which it is clear that it is better to speak of the "Life of the Fathers" rather than the "Lives of the Fathers", the more so since there is a diversity of merits and virtues among them, but the one life of the body sustains them all in this world. I have indeed related, more briefly, some facts about the life of some of these men in my book on the Confessors, below;[3] things which may be reckoned great by the power of God are made small by my writing. But in this present work, which we have decided to call the *Life of the Saints*, we have presumed, despite our inexperience and ignorance, to speak of these things at greater length, praying to the Lord that He may put words in our mouth, as He has often rendered speech to the dumb, so that my lips may utter things salutary to my hearers and readers, and worthy of the holy fathers; and the things which He instructs me to write on the saints, may He regard them as sung in His own praise.

---

1. Aulus Gellius, a second-century grammarian, and author of a miscellany, *Noctes Atticae*: for this comment see I 3 1 and XIII 2 1. Most manuscripts of *VP* have Agellius; no. 4 has A. Gellius. For a comment on this grammatical discussion, see my introduction, p. xiv.

2. The grammatical books of Pliny the Elder (died AD 79, in the same Vesuvian eruption that destroyed Pompeii) do not survive: Pliny mentions them himself in the Preface to his *Natural History*.

3. The order of the Eight Books of Miracles is *GM*; *VSJ*; *VSM* I-IV; *VP*; *GC*. In the preface to *GC* Gregory says "[I wrote] four books about the miracles of St Martin, and a seventh [*VP*] about the life of some blessed [saints]. I am writing this eighth book about the miracles of the confessors" (transl. Van Dam, p. 17). For the actual order of writing, see my introduction, p. xii.

I.   About the saints Lupicinus and Romanus, abbots

The order of evangelical discipline tells us that the money of Our Lord's largesse, when placed with the money-changers, will, with God's favour, obtain a just and fruitful multiplication, and that it must not remain hidden to corrode and rot away in deep pits, but should be put to a rational use and grow into profit in the winning of eternal life; then, when the Lord comes to ask about the sum that He has lent, He may say, while taking the interest from His loan with double satisfaction, "Well done, good and faithful servant; thou hast been faithful over a few things, I will make thee ruler over many things: enter thou into the joy of the Lord" (Matthew 25:23). It belongs indeed to the predestined to accomplish these things with the help of the Lord; they have merited the knowledge of the Lord from the time they wailed in the cradle, as one reads of many, and, having known Him, they have never deviated from His precepts and, after the sacrament of baptism, they have never soiled by shameful acts the white and shining robe of regeneration. Deservedly they follow the Lamb wherever He leads, the Lamb whose great whiteness has crowned them with beautiful lilies, not withered by the heat of any temptation. In presenting these crowns the right hand of Divine Majesty encourages those who start, aids those who are winning, rewards the victorious, and raises those marked in advance by His Name from the groanings of the earth, lifting them up, glorious, to the joys of Heaven. I do not doubt that among the number of the chosen, clad in white, are those who shine in the darkness of the Jura desert, who have not only deserved to become the temple of the Lord themselves, but who have also in the souls of many others prepared the tabernacles of the grace of the Holy Spirit: I speak of Lupicinus and Romanus, his brother.[1]

---

1. The lives of Romanus and Lupicinus, together with the abbot who succeeded them, Eugendus, are related in the *Vita Patrum Jurensium* or *Iurensium* (*VPJ*), written by a monk at one of the Jura monasteries for John and Armentarius, who were apparently monks at St-Maurice-d'Agaune: see F. Martine, *Vie des Pères du Jura* (Sources Chrétiennes 142, Paris 1968) for a text, French translation, notes and commentary. (It also contains a text and translation of *VP* I, on pp. 446-61.) For the best account in English of the Jura monasteries in their context see Wood 1981. A number of scholars, including Krusch (*MGH SSRM* III 125-9), have argued for a date of the ninth century or later for *VPJ*, but it now seems agreed that the text dates from not long after the death of the

1. Lupicinus sought God with all his heart from his earliest years. He was instructed in letters, but then, having reached a suitable age, he was forced by his father, without his consent, into the bonds of betrothal.[2] But Romanus, who was still too young, desired to consecrate his soul to the service of God, and refused to marry. When their parents died, they both with common accord desire the desert. They go together into the depths of the Jura wilderness, between Burgundia and Alamannia, in an area adjacent to the city of Avenches.[3] There they build huts, and every day, prostrate upon the ground, they address their prayers to the Lord with a melodious chanting of psalms; their only nourishment is the roots of plants. But the malice of the one who fell from Heaven has always laid traps for mankind, and he attacks these servants of God and strives, with the help of his ministers, to call them back from the road which they have taken. For every day without

---

author's abbot and informant, Eugendus, in c.510. F. Masai would date its composition to shortly before 515: see "La Vita patrum iurensium et les débuts du monachisme à Saint-Maurice d'Agaune', in *Festschrift Bernhard Bischoff zu seinem 65. Geburtstag* (Stuttgart, 1971), 43-69; Martine suggests c.520 (pp. 55-57, at the end of a detailed discussion of the question of authenticity, pp. 14-57).

There are numerous differences between *VP* I and *VPJ*. Gregory's account leaves out much of the detail, and the two disagree crucially on a number of points (see notes 2, 3, 8, 9, 10 below). Clearly Gregory could not have known *VPJ*. But there are a few similarities in the words used in the two accounts: "at the most we may admit that Gregory of Tours used a very poor and unreliable summary of *VPJ*, or else that the two authors had access to the same old and brief account of the two monastic founders" (Martine, p. 73).

2. This is not mentioned in *VPJ*, which says that Lupicinus was the younger of the two: I 3 (Martine pp. 252-3). Martine suggests (p. 265) that it was Lupicinus' vigour and authority, and the length of his life (about twenty years longer than that of Romanus), which made Gregory, a century later, think of him as the elder and leader.

3. The Jura mountains, in the west of the territory of Avenches, in fact formed a frontier zone between the territory controlled by the Burgundians and that controlled by the Alamans. In this translation *civitas* is normally rendered "city", meaning the entire territory around the urban centre: it can be equivalent to "diocese". According to *VPJ*, Romanus, in his 35th year (around 435, says Martine, p. 11), went alone to the Jura wilderness, "having left his mother, his sister and his brother" (I 1, Martine pp. 244-5). It was only at a later date that Lupicinus joined him. Gregory, when he has both brothers going out together, may have been confused, as Duchesne suggested, by some memory of the two other brothers who came together from Nyon to join Romanus' monastery: *VPJ* I 3, Martine pp. 254-5.

ceasing demons threw stones at them, and every time they bent their knees to pray to the Lord, immediately a shower of stones thrown by demons fell on them, in such a way that they were often wounded and endured atrocious torments.[4] And their youth (for they had not yet reached maturity) began to fear those daily attacks of the Enemy; not being able to support these torments any longer, they resolve to leave the desert and return home. To what can the envy of the Enemy not drive us? Abandoning their home which they had desired so much, and returning to the habitations of men, they enter the house of a poor woman. She asks the soldiers of Christ where they have come from. They reply, not without embarrassment, that they have left the wilderness, and they tell in detail what had turned them away from their purpose. Then she says to them: "O men of God, you should have fought bravely against the wiles of the Devil, and not feared the enmity of him who has so often been laid low, overcome by the friends of God. He is envious of sanctity, for he fears that the human race, whose fall he brought about by his perfidy, will rise again ennobled by its faith." And they, touched to the heart, withdrew from the woman, and said "Woe on us, for we have sinned against the Lord by abandoning our purpose. Behold, we are convinced of our cowardice by a woman! What will the end of our life be if we do not return to those places from which we have been expelled by the shaft of the Enemy?"

2. Then, armed by the sign of the Cross, their sticks in hand, they returned to the desert. On their arrival the treacherous demons began to renew their stone-throwing, but they, persisting in prayer, obtained God's favour, so that the temptation was removed and they could persevere freely and unimpeded in the worship of their Lord. While they were occupied in prayer, crowds of brothers began to flock to them from all sides, to hear the word of preaching from them. And when the blessed hermits were, as we have said, known to people, they

---

4. For an excellent discussion on the role of the Devil and demons in late antique hagiography, see Stancliffe 1983, esp. pp. 193-5, where she discusses the symbolic use of the devil in Christian literature, "when the writer was well aware that it was a human agent who was immediately responsible for the deed in question, and is simply using 'devil' as a shorthand for 'a man acting under demoniacal inspiration'" (p. 194).

built a monastery which they called Condat.[5] There they cleared the forest and made fields, and obtained food for themselves by their own manual labour. So great a fervour of the love of God had filled the inhabitants of the region that the crowds assembled for the service of the Lord were too great to be assembled in one place; thus they built another monastery, where they established a swarm from the blessed hive.[6] Then, with the help of God, this new congregation grew also, and they built a third monastery in Alamannia.[7]

These two fathers went in turn to visit their children, whom they had filled with divine knowledge, preaching in each monastery the truths necessary for the formation of their souls. Lupicinus nevertheless obtained the sole power over them with the title of abbot. He was very sober, and abstained from eating and drinking, so that often he took food only once every three days. And when the necessity of the human body caused him to be thirsty, he had brought to him a jar full of water, in which he immersed his hands for a long time. A marvellous thing! His flesh absorbed the water, so that you would have thought that he had swallowed it with his mouth: thus he quenched his thirst. He was very severe in the punishment of the brothers; far from permitting them to act wrongly, he did not even allow them to speak wrongly. He very carefully avoided any discourse or meeting with women. Romanus, on the other hand, was so simple that none of these severities came to his mind; after having invoked the name of God he gave equally to men and to women the blessings which they sought.

3. Abbot Lupicinus did not have enough resources to sustain such a large community; God revealed to him a place in the desert in which treasures had been hidden in ancient times. He went to this place

---

5. *Condatiscone monasterium*, which was later known as *St Eugendi Iurense* and modernised to Saint-Oyan-de-Joux: it is now Saint-Claude (dép. Jura). See V-T no. 241 and, for a few comments on the buildings, James 1981 p. 36.

6. *Lauconnum*, now Saint-Lupicin (dép. Jura).

7. Probably *Romani monasterium*, now Romainmôtier (cant. Vaud). For this identification see the discussion in M. Besson, *Recherches sur les origines des évêchés de Genève, Lausanne et Sion et leurs premiers titulaires jusqu' au déclin du VIe siècle* (Fribourg-Paris, 1906), pp. 210-27). The earliest church found in excavations probably dates from the refounding by Columbanian monks in the seventh century: see V-T no. 230.

on his own, and brought back as much gold and silver as he could carry
to the monastery. Buying food with it, he nourished the crowds of
brothers whom he had assembled to serve God. He used to do this each
year, and he did not reveal to any of the brothers the place which the
Lord had shown to him.

It happened one day that he was visiting those of the brothers
who, as we said, had assembled in the region of Alamannia.[8] He
arrived at midday, when the brothers were still in the fields, and entered
the building in which the food was being cooked for the meal; he saw
there a great array of different dishes, and a pile of fish, and he said to
himself, "it is not right that monks, whose life is solitary, should have
such unsuitable luxuries." And he ordered a great copper cauldron to be
prepared, and when it had started to heat on the fire he put in it all the
prepared dishes, fish, vegetables and beans, and everything else prepared
for the monks, and mixed them all together, and then he said, "Now the
monks can eat their fill of this stew, for they will not abandon
themselves to pleasure which could turn them away from their divine
calling." When the monks heard this they were very discontented.
Twelve men discussed it together, and they left the monastery in a rage
and went out to wander through the wilderness in search of the
pleasures of the world. Romanus learnt of this immediately, by means
of a vision, for divine mercy did not want him to remain ignorant of
what had happened. When Abbot Lupicinus returned to the monastery,
Romanus said to him, "If you left here just so that you could drive
monks away, it would have been better if you had stayed behind!" The
abbot replied, "Do not be angry over what has happened, dearest
brother. Know that the threshing-floor of the Lord has been purified,

8. *VPJ* tells the same story (if it is the same story) quite differently, at I 13 (Martine pp.
278-85). The gentle Romanus was unable to stop some of the gourmet monks at Condat
(not the monastery in Alamannia) from indulging themselves, and calls in his more
rigorous brother from Lauconnum. After a couple of days of the more normal fare,
Lupicinus cheerfully suggests meals of unseasoned porridge. No-one dares protest. But
when he suggests that he might change places with Romanus so that he could stay on at
Condat to enjoy the fine porridge, the gourmets decide to leave. Despite the different
accounts, both authors use the same unusual word of these monks: Gregory calls them
cotornosi atque elati and the anonymous author of *VPJ* says *cothurnositate superbos* (after
cothurnus, the high-soled buskin of the tragic actor, a symbol of grandeur and majesty,
and hence of pride).

and that the wheat alone remains for placing in the granary: the chaff
has been thrown away." And Romanus said, "It would have been better
if no brothers had departed! Tell me, I beg you, how many did leave?"
"Twelve men", replied the abbot, "men vain and proud, in whom God
does not dwell." And Romanus, weeping, said "I believe, from what I
know of divine mercy, that the Lord will not separate them from his
treasure, but will reunite them and gain those for whom He suffered."
And having prayed for them, he obtained that they might return to the
grace of Almighty God. And the Lord did indeed touch their hearts with
remorse, and, doing penance for their departure, they each assembled
their own communities and founded their own monasteries, which
persevere to this day in praising God. And Romanus continued in his
simplicity and good works, visiting the sick and curing them by his
prayers.

4. It happened one day, while on the way to visit his brothers,
that he was overtaken by nightfall, and turned aside into a house of
lepers. There were nine men there.[9] Having been welcomed by them,
immediately, full of the love of God, he ordered water to be heated and
with his own hand he washed the feet of all of them. Then he had a
large bed prepared so that they could all rest together on one couch,
without any fear for the livid spots of leprosy. That done, while the
lepers slept, Romanus, awake and chanting psalms, stretched out his
hand and touched the side of one of the sick men, and immediately he
was cleansed; he touched another with healing touch, and that one too
was immediately cleansed. These men felt themselves restored to health,
and each touched his neighbour, and when they had all thus been
awakened, they begged the saint to cure them. But by the touches they
had given each other they had already been cured. In the morning
Romanus saw that all shone with the freshness of their skin. He gave
thanks to God, took his leave of each of them with a kiss, and departed,
recommending to them that they keep those things pertaining to God in
their hearts, and put them into practice.

5. Lupicinus, now an old man, went to find King Chilperic,

---

9. But only two, father and son, in *VPJ* I 15 (Martine pp. 290-1).

who then ruled Burgundy, for he had heard that he was living in the town of Geneva.[10] When he went through the gateway, the king, who was at his dinner-table, felt his throne shake. He was frightened, and said to those around him, "There's been an earthquake!" They replied that they had not felt any shaking. And the king said, "Go quickly to the gate, in case there is anyone there who desires our kingdom, or wishes to harm us; for this throne has shaken for a reason." They ran immediately to the gate, and found an old man covered in clothes of skin. They announced this to the king, who said "Go, bring him into my presence, so that I may know what kind of a man he is." Lupicinus was led in and stood before the king, just like Jacob before Pharaoh. Chilperic said to him, "Who are you? Where do you come from? What is your business, or what necessity do you lack, that you come to me? Speak!" Lupicinus replied, "I am the father of the Lord's sheep. The Lord nourishes them with spiritual food, under the yoke of discipline, but they now lack bodily food. This is why we implore Your Potency that you might give us something for our food and clothing." The king replied, "Take fields and vineyards, so that you can live and satisfy your needs." He replied, "We will not accept fields and vines; but, if it

---

10. This Chilperic was Chilperic I, king of the Burgundians in the 460s and 470s: the author of *VPJ* gives him his Roman titles *vir illuster* and *patricius Galliae* (II 10: Martine p. 336), adding that at this time "public authority had passed under a royal régime". In *VPJ* the visit to Chilperic was made on behalf of poor people who were being oppressed by a palace official. Gregory has no echo of the diatribe which *VPJ* puts into the mouth of Lupicinus; *VPJ* does not mention the favours which the king bestowed on the Jura monasteries. Martine dates this visit to Geneva to c.467 (p. 337 n.3).

Chilperic was probably the brother of Gundioc and uncle of the later kings, Chilperic II and Gundobad: on him see *PLRE* 2 pp. 286-7 and Heinzelmann 1982 p. 580. This text shows him in court at Geneva (where the praetorium building which he must have used has been excavated by L. Blondel: see his *Praetorium, palais burgonde et château comtal* (Geneva 1940) and "Les monuments burgondes à Genève", *Bull. Soc. Hist. Arch. Genève*, ii (1958), pp. 211-58). A few years later, in 471-2, he was resident at Lyons which appears to have been the other major Burgundian royal residence. As Wood has pointed out (Wood 1977 pp. 20-1), he appears in the sources (e.g. *VPJ* or Sidonius Apollinaris, *Epist.* VI 12; V 6; V 7) as a Roman imperial official rather than a Burgundian king. It is significant that here Gregory, unlike *VPJ*, simply bestows on him the title of king, the constitutional niceties of the fifth century being long forgotten: cf. the case of the Roman official Syagrius, referred to as *rex Romanorum* in *LH* I 27, on whom see E. James, "Childéric, Syagrius et la disparition du royaume de Soissons", *Revue Archéologique de Picardie* 1988 (3-4), p. 11 and James 1988, p. 71.

pleases Your Potency, give us some of the fruits that they produce. It does not suit monks to live by worldly riches; they ought rather to find in the humility of their heart the kingdom of God and His justice." The king heard these words, and gave them an order to receive each year 300 modii of wheat and the same measure of wine, and 100 gold solidi for clothing for the brothers. Even now they receive all this, it is said, from the estates of the fisc.

6. Later, when Abbot Lupicinus and Romanus were old men advanced in age, Lupicinus said to his brother, "Tell me, in which monastery do you want your burial place to be prepared, so that we may rest together?" Romanus replied, "I do not want to have my tomb in a monastery, which women are forbidden to enter. As you know, the Lord has given me the grace of bringing cures, although I am unworthy and do not deserve it, and many have been snatched from various illnesses by the imposition of my hands and the power of the Lord's cross. Thus many people will gather at my tomb when I leave the light of this life. That is why I ask to rest far from the monastery." For that reason, when he died he was buried ten miles from the monastery, on a small hill.[11] At length a great church was built over the tomb, and large crowds came there every day. Many miracles are now accomplished there in the name of God: the blind find the light, the deaf their hearing, the paralysed the use of their limbs. Abbot Lupicinus was buried in the basilica of the monastery,[12] and he thus left to the Lord greatly multiplied the sums which had been lent to him, that is to say, the blessed congregations of monks devoted to His praise.

---

11. According to *VPJ* (I 19, Martine pp. 304-5), Romanus was buried at *Balma*, La Balme, a large nunnery whose abbess was his sister. The site is described in detail in *VPJ* I 9 (Martine pp. 264-7).

12. Of Lauconnum, according to *VPJ* II 16 (Martine pp. 360-63).

II.   About St Illidius, a confessor

Among the other seeds of perpetual life with which the heavenly Sower has from the fountain of His divinity watered the field of the untutored soul with His precepts and fertilised it with His teaching, He says: "And he that taketh not his cross and followeth me, is not worthy of me" (Matthew 10:38). And that elect vessel, the blessed apostle Paul, has he not said, "Always bear about in the body the dying of the Lord Jesus, that the life also of Jesus might be made manifest in your mortal body" (II Corinth. 4:10)? Therefore the confessors of Christ, whom the time of persecution has not provoked to martyrdom, have become their own persecutors, in order to be thought worthy of God. They have charged themselves with various crosses of abstinence, and in order to live with Jesus Christ they have mortified their flesh, following the words of the Apostle: "It is not I who live, but Christ liveth in me" (Galat. 2:20). For they saw by the eyes of their inner understanding that the Lord of the Heavens came down to earth, not abased by humility, but humiliated by His mercy, for the redemption of the world; they saw hanging from the cross, not the glory of the Divinity, but the pure sacrifice of the body which He had taken on, as St John had foreseen shortly before: "Behold the Lamb of God, which taketh away the sin of the world" (John 1:29). They had in them the mark of the nails when, transfixed by fear of Him and filled with terror of the judgements of God, they did not have within the habitation of their heart anything unworthy of His power. In them shone that bright light of the resurrection, with which the angel glittered when he removed the stone from the tomb; Jesus was thus resplendent when he entered (unexpectedly, for the doors were closed) into the midst of the assembly of the apostles, and also when, after filling them with the words of life, he was raised up to the celestial heights. The blessed confessor Illidius so placed all these things in the tabernacle of his heart that he too might deserve to become a temple of the Holy Spirit.

As I prepare to write something of his life, I beg the indulgence of my readers. I have indeed not made any study of grammar, and I have not been polished by the cultivated reading of secular writers; instead the blessed father Avitus, bishop of Clermont, exhorted me to study ecclesiastical works.[1] If the things which I have heard in his sermons or that he has got me to read have not formed my judgement, although I cannot observe them, it is he, second only to the psalms of David, who has led me to the words of evangelical preaching, and to the stories and epistles of apostolic virtue; it is from him that I have been able to know that Jesus Christ, the Son of God, came for the salvation of the world, and to honour by worthy homage His friends who, taking the cross of an austere observance, have followed the Bridegroom. And now, having displayed all the temerity of my rustic ignorance, I am going to tell as well as I can what I have learnt of the blessed Illidius.

1. The holy Illidius, who recommended himself by perfect sanctity of life and who accumulated in himself the gift of diverse graces bestowed on him by God, merited what until then had not been granted to his already lofty sanctity: he was chosen, by the inspiration of God and the choice of the people, as bishop of the church of Clermont and pastor of the Lord's sheep.[2] The renown of his holiness, elevated by various degrees of grace, extended not only into all parts of the Auvergne, but even crossed the frontiers into neighbouring towns. Finally the rumour of his glory came to the ears of the emperor at Trier, whose daughter suffered much, being possessed by a devil; no-one could be found to cast it out.[3] Illidius was recommended by popular rumour. Immediately the emperor sent messengers, who speedily brought the holy old man to Trier by royal authority. He is received

---

1. Avitus was bishop of Clermont from c.572 to c.594. Gregory's intellectual debt to Avitus (when the latter was archdeacon) is mentioned in Venantius Fortunatus' poem on Avitus' conversion of the Jews in Clermont, addressed to Gregory: *Carm.* V 5 143-8: "It is not enough for you yourself to praise his virtues; you compel others to praise them too. It was not in vain that he raised you up as a pupil, for your heart has remained faithful to him and you return the love which he showed you. May God grant that for generations to come you give praise to him, and he to you." The conversion of the Jews is related by Gregory at *LH* V 11, and discussed in Brennan 1985 and Goffart 1985. On Gregory's lack of grammatical knowledge, cf. my introduction, pp. xviii-xix.

2. He succeeded Legonus, according to Gregory, *LH* I 45, where Gregory refers to *VP* II.

3. The emperor is Maximus (383-88), who also plays an important role in Sulpicius Severus' *Life of St Martin*.

with great respect by the ruler, who is very troubled by the unhappy plight of his daughter. The holy bishop, trusting in the Lord, prostrates himself in prayer. He passed an entire night singing sacred hymns and songs, and then put his fingers into the mouth of the young girl and chased out the evil spirit which had tormented her body. The emperor sees this miracle, and offers the holy bishop great heaps of gold and silver. He vehemently refused this gift, but he asked for and obtained that the city of the Auvergne, which paid tribute in kind, in wheat and wine, should pay it in gold, for it was only with great trouble that the tribute in kind could be transported to the imperial treasury.[4] The saint fulfilled the time of his earthly life, and left on that speedy journey towards Christ; his body was carried off by his own people and buried in his town.[5]

2. Since people are very accustomed to criticise, someone will perhaps foolishly say, "It is not possible for a man to be ranked among the saints just for this one miracle." But one should weigh well what the Lord says in the Gospel, "Many will say to me in that day, Lord, Lord, have we not cast out devils in thy name? and in thy name done many wonderful works? and then will I profess unto them, I never knew you" (Matthew 7:22-3). Assuredly He means that [the virtue which comes from the tomb is much more worthy of praise than those things which a living person has worked in this world] because the latter could be blemished by the continual difficulties of worldly occupations, while the former were certainly free from all blemish. And since, as we believe, the deeds done by St Illidius before his death have been forgotten and have not come to our knowledge, we will tell what we have seen with our own eyes, what we have experienced, or what we have learnt from

---

4. Tax-commutation of this kind was common from the late fourth century onwards: see Jones 1964 p. 460. Perhaps the story came about in order to explain why the Auvergne paid taxes in this manner. Cf. also C. Wickham, "The other transition: from the ancient world to feudalism", *Past and Present*, 103 (1984), pp. 3-36, at p. 10.

5. He died in either 384 or 385, since Nepotianus was bishop of Clermont at the synod of Trier in 385. His death was celebrated on June 5; his tomb had a basilica built over it, probably in the fifth century, which was enlarged by Avitus in the 570s or 580s and survived until its burning by Pippin in 761. For some sculptural survivals from the church of St-Allyre, see V-T, no. 75.

trustworthy people.

At the time when Gallus governed the church of Clermont, the author of these words, still a boy, was seriously ill; and he was often visited by the bishop, who loved him much, and was indeed his uncle.[6] His stomach was filled with a great quantity of phlegm, and he was seized by a very strong fever. Then there came to the child a desire which, I believe, came from God, that he might be carried to the church of the blessed Illidius. He was carried by servants to the tomb of the saint, and, mingling prayers with his tears, he felt much more at ease than he had before. But when he returned home he was again taken by the fever. Then, one day when he found himself even more ill and when the fever was stronger than usual, to the point that it was thought that he would never recover, his mother came to him and said, "Today, my sweet son, I will be full of sadness, for you are so ill." And he replied, "Please don't be sad, but send me to the tomb of the blessed bishop Illidius, for I believe and I trust that his virtue will find happiness for you and health for me". And so he was taken to the tomb of the saint, and he addressed a prayer to the Lord, freely promising that if he were delivered of his sickness by the intercession of the bishop, he would at once become a cleric. Hardly had he spoken when he felt his fever begin to leave him; he called his servant and asked to be taken home. There he was put to bed, and while the house was at table, he had a great nose-bleed, and as the blood flowed the fever left him. This was certainly obtained by the merits of the blessed confessor. Recently also a servant of Count Venerandus,[7] after having been blind for a long time, celebrated vigils near the tomb and returned cured.

3. As for what has happened with his relics, this is what the same writer has seen with his own eyes. He had dedicated an oratory in the bishop's house at Tours, in the first year of his episcopate, in which

---

6. Gallus was bishop from c.525 to 551; for his life, see below, *VP* VI, and for the role of Gallus and his family in ecclesiastical politics in Clermont, see Wood 1983. He was Gregory's uncle, the brother of Gregory's father Florentius.

7. The count of Clermont, possibly the successor to Firminus: see Selle-Horsbach 1974, p. 163.

he put the relics of this holy bishop together with those of other saints.[8]
A long time after the dedication he was warned by the abbot to check
the relics which he had placed in the altar, for fear that the humidity of
the new building had caused them to moulder. He did indeed find them
to be damp, and so he took them from the altar and began to dry them
at a fire. And he wrapped them each up in turn, and then came to the
relics of the blessed bishop Illidius, and held them to the fire. The string
which bound them was too long, and fell onto the burning coals: like
copper or iron it began to redden in the heart of the fire. Not worrying
much about the string as long as the sacred relics were dried properly,
he thought that it would have been burnt up in the flames; nevertheless
when he draws it out the string is unharmed. Seeing this he is
astonished, and marvels at the power of this truly blessed bishop. And
it was not without great fear that he brought away news of this deed,
and revealed his glory to all. The string in question was made of wool.

4.[9]   There was a little boy of about ten months who was
gener-ally recognised to be the great-grandson of the blessed man. This
child was afflicted by a very grave illness. The mother wept, not so
much for the death of the child as for the fact that he had not yet been
anointed by the sacrament of baptism. Finally, having taken advice, she
went to the tomb of the blessed confessor, laid the sick child, who
barely breathed, on the ground, and kept watch with vigils and prayers
in front of the saint's tomb. Then, as the bird which announces the
coming of day sang loudly and beat its wings, the child, who had been
stretched out unconscious, awoke and shows by a laugh the joy of his
heart; he opened his mouth and calls his mother, saying, "Come here!"
She comes, full of fear as well as joy, for she had never heard the voice
of her son before, and she was amazed. "What do you want," she says,
"my own sweet son?" He replies, "Go quickly, and bring me a cup of
water." But she remained motionless in prayer until daybreak, giving
thanks to the holy bishop and consecrating her son to him; then she
went into the house. The child drank the water which was given to him

---

8. Including the relics of Saturninus, Julian and Martin, according to *GC* 20; of Stephen,
according to *GM* 33; and of the pallium which had wrapped up the True Cross, *GM* 5. See
V-T, no. 310. The first year of Gregory's episcopate was 573/4.

9. The text of this chapter is found intact only in manuscript 4.

and, delivered from all infirmity, he recovered his health. Then he returned to the first wailings of infancy, and never spoke again until he reached that age at which children are accustomed to loosen their tongues in speech.

I do not think that I should be silent about what happened once when a furnace was lit to heat the lime for the church. The lintel which strengthened the opening of the furnace broke, while all those who were there, including the abbot of the place, were asleep. At that moment the abbot saw in a dream a bishop who said to him, "Hasten to awake those who sleep, in case the imminent collapse harms anyone. The lintel which holds up the mass of stones is about to fall into the fire." The abbot awoke, and made everyone stand clear of the entrance to the furnace, and the mass of stones fell on both sides without hurting anyone, which would not have happened, I think, without the intervention of the bishop. Then the abbot, after having prayed at the tomb of the saint, had the supports repaired and the stones replaced, and the work of the furnace could begin again, thanks to the bishop.

The blessed body of the confessor had formerly been buried in a crypt, but, as the building was narrow and difficult of access, St Avitus, bishop of the town, had built an apse of circular shape and admirable workmanship, and sought for the blessed bones, finding them in a coffin made of wooden planks. He took them up, wrapped them up in a suitable linen cloth, and, according to custom, enclosed them in a sarcophagus; he filled up the crypt and placed the sarcophagus at a higher level. In this place also Justus lies, a man just in both name and deed, who is said to have been the archdeacon of this glorious pontiff.[10]

5. There are many other miracles reported of this same saint, which I thought would be too long to relate; I think that what I have said will suffice for a perfect faith, since the man for whom little things are not enough will not be convinced by great things. In fact, at the

---

10. This information about Justus is repeated in *LH* I 45. It is clear from the tenth-century *Libellus de ecclesiis Claromontanis* (ed. Levison, *MGH SSRM* VII pp. 454-67), 11, that St Allyre became an important episcopal funerary basilica: bishops Gallus, Desideratus and Avolus were among those buried here, as well as the two chaste lovers whose tombs miraculously came together — see *LH* I 47 and *Libellus*, 11.

tomb of the saint the blind are given light, demons are chased away, the deaf receive hearing and the lame the use of their limbs, by the grace of Our Lord Jesus Christ, who promises to believers that He will give to those who ask and who do not doubt the success of their prayers.

III.   About St Abraham, an abbot

I do not believe that there is a catholic who does not know that the Lord says in the Gospel: "Verily I say unto you, if ye have faith and doubt not, and if you say to this mountain, Be thou removed; it shall be done" (Matthew 21:21). And "All that you ask in my name, believe that you will receive it and it will come to you" (Mark 11:23). There is no reason to doubt that the saints can obtain from the Lord whatever they ask, because the faith which is in them is solid and cannot be shaken by the waves of hesitation. And in this faith not only have they been banned from their own country because they desired to lead a celestial life, but they have even gone to foreign countries beyond the sea, in order more to please Him to whom they have committed their lives.

Such was the case in our days with the blessed abbot Abraham, who after many temptations of the world made his way to the Auvergne. And it is not without good reason that he is compared in the greatness of his faith to that old man Abraham, to whom God had said, "Get thee out of thy country, and from thy kindred, unto a land that I will shew thee" (Genesis 12:1). And he left not only his own country, but also the life of the Old Man, and he put on the New Man, formed according to God in justice, holiness and truth. This is why, when he saw himself perfect in the work of God, he did not hesitate in his faith to search for what he was confident of obtaining by a holy life, and through him the Author of Heaven, of the sea and of earth deigned to work miracles — not numerous indeed, but worthy of admiration.

1. This Abraham, then, was born on the banks of the river Euphrates, where, advanced in the work of God, he conceived the desire to go into the wilderness of Egypt to visit the hermits. On the way he was taken by pagans and after having taken a great number of blows in the name of Jesus Christ, he was thrown into prison. He languished there for five years, until he was delivered by an angel. Desiring then to visit western shores, he came to the Auvergne, and established a

monastery near the church of St Cyricus.[1] He had a marvellous virtue for driving our demons, giving sight to the blind, and curing other maladies. Then, when the feast of this church had come, he told the prior to prepare a jar of wine, as usual, in the forecourt of the church, for the refreshment of the people who were at the ceremonies. The monk complained, saying, "Look, you've invited the bishop, the duke and the citizens, and there are scarcely four jars of wine left. Where are we going to get enough wine for all those people?" And he replied, "Open the cellar!" That was done, and he entered and prays, like a new Elijah, lifting his hands to heaven, with his eyes full of tears:[2] "O Lord, I pray that wine shall not be lacking in this jar until all have received an abundance." And he is filled with the Holy Spirit, and cries, "Thus saith the Lord: the wine shall not lack in this jar, but all those who ask for it shall have enough, and there shall be an abundance left over."[3] And it happened as he had said: it was served in profusion to all the people, who drank of it happily, and there was wine left over. The conscientious prior had previously measured the jar, which was a size to contain 50 measures, and had found that it contained only four hands; seeing what had happened he measured it again the following day, and found that there was as much wine in the jar as before. The power of the saint was thus made manifest to all. He finally died, at a great age, in the monastery, and he was buried there with honour. At that time Sidonius was bishop and the duke was Victorius, who had received the principality of seven cities by the will of Euric, king of the Goths.[4] The

---

1. He was abbot in Clermont at the time of Duke Victorius and Bishop Sidonius, thus between 475 and 484, Gregory mentions him in this context in *LH* II 21, where he refers to "the book of his life which I have written" (i.e. *VP* III). St Cirgues is some 600 m from the walls of Clermont, near the baptistery: see V-T no. 81.

2. A reference to the miracle performed by Elijah, I Kings 17:14 ff.

3. An echo of Matthew 25:29.

4. Sidonius is the best-known bishop of fifth-century Gaul, thanks to his poems and ten books of letters: on him see *LH* II 21-22, *PLRE* 2 pp 115-118 and C.E. Stevens, *Sidonius Apollinaris and His Age* (Oxford, 1933).
   On Duke Victorius see *PLRE* 2 pp. 1162-4. He was given the seven cities in the 14th year of Euric's reign, according to *LH* II 20, therefore in 470: on the other hand, Gregory's chronology is not too trustworthy, for in the same chapter he credits Euric (466-484) with 27 years of reign. Gregory gives Victorius credit for his church-building (see below, n. 24 to *VP* VI), but objects to his morals (he accused him of murdering the

blessed Sidonius composed the epitaph for our saint, where he has mentioned some of the things we have related.[5] Many people with fevers have slept by the tomb of the blessed Abraham and have been cured with the aid of heavenly remedies.

---

senator Eucherius, and of having affairs with women). He fled to Rome with Sidonius Apollinaris' son (see *PLRE* 2 p. 114), and was stoned to death: this happened after he had been duke for nine years, says Gregory. Abraham died before that, as Sidonius Apollinaris says that Victorius was at Abraham's death-bed (*Epist.* VII 17): therefore his death was before 479. His feast-day is June 15. The church of St Cirgues (see above n.1), where his monastery was, not far from St Illidius's church (St Allyre) in Clermont, preserved his tomb in the tenth century, according to the *Libellus de ecclesiis Claromontanis* (ed. Levison, *MGH SSRM* VII pp. 454-67), 14.

5. See Sidonius Apollinaris, *Epist.* VII 17. In c.477 Sidonius, bishop of Clermont wrote to "his brother" Volusianus, saying that he would contribute a verse epitaph for Abraham "moved alike by your authority and even more by the devotion of the noble Count Victorius ... He has insisted on taking the funeral almost entirely upon himself and defraying all the expenses required for the due obsequies of a priest". The epitaph itself gives a brief biography which conforms to Gregory's picture. "Born by the Euphrates, for Christ thou didst endure the prison, chains, and hunger for five long years. From the cruel King of Susa [the pagan referred to by Gregory is thus the Persian ruler] thou didst fly, escaping alone to the distant land of the West. Marvels born of his holiness followed the steps of the confessor; thyself a fugitive thou didst put to flight the spirit of evil. Wherever thy footsteps passed, the throng of lemures [kinless ghosts] cried surrender; the exile's voice bade the demons go forth into banishment. All sought thee, yet didst thou yield to no vain ambition; the honours acceptable in thy sight were those that brought the heaviest burdens ...". In return Sidonius requested that the bishop place Abraham's monks, "now cast adrift without a leader", under a monastic rule drawn from the monasteries of Lérins or Grigny: he also suggests that Auxanius should be their abbot. (I quote from the translation of O.M. Dalton [Oxford, 1915], II pp. 133-6.) In fact Volusianus may have become abbot of St Cirgues after Abraham, and may be the same Volusianus who succeeded Perpetuus as bishop of Tours in 488: see A. Loyen, *Sidoine Apollinaire: Tome III* (Paris, 1970), p. 195.

IV.   About St Quintianus

Every man who knows that he possesses a body made of terrestrial matter must be careful that terrestrial and fleshly things do not become dear to him, because, as St Paul said, "the works of the flesh are manifest" (Galat. 5:19), full of impurity, rendering men who indulge in them polluted and unclean, and dooming them at the last to eternal weeping. The fruit of the Spirit is all that profits and shines in God, all that here below exalts the soul by the mortification of the flesh and assures it of eternal joy in the future. Thus we who are now placed in the body must watch what God has accomplished in His saints, dwelling in whom as in a splendid, white and smooth tabernacle garlanded with the flowers of their diverse merits He has stretched out the majesty of His right hand and has deigned in His mercy to accomplish through them what they ask for. We see this in the blessed Quintianus, of whom we shall speak, a person remarkable by his generosity and nobility of spirit, in whom the Lord has fulfilled the work of His justice. Therefore let not a striving after the things of the flesh submerge and lower us like beasts, but rather, following the saints and understanding wisely the things of God, may He lift us towards celestial and heavenly things; and may our mind not wallow in sin, conquered by shameful deeds, but let wisdom reign victorious, defending her throne for the benefits of eternity.

1. The blessed Quintianus, an African (and, as some say, the nephew of Bishop Faustus who, it is reported, had raised his mother from the dead),[1] was a person endowed with sanctity, resplendent with virtue, heated by the fire of charity, and adorned with the flower of chastity: he was chosen bishop of Rodez, he was sought for, he was consecrated.[2] In this episcopacy his virtues increased, and as he

---

1. It is not clear who Faustus is, although it could be the Faustus Praesidiensis mentioned in Victor of Vita's *Life of St Fulgentius*, I.38.

2. As bishop of Rodez he attended the Visigothic council of Agde in 506 and the Frankish Council of Orleans in 511: this proves that Gregory's dating of his expulsion to the period before 507 in *LH* II 36 is false: see n. 4 below. Rodez, taken by the Franks before 511, seems to have fallen into Visigothic hands afterwards; it is not surprising that a bishop who had attended the first great "national" Frankish church council in 511 should

advanced in the works of the Lord he enlarged the church of the blessed bishop Amantius and has his body taken there.[3] But the saint was not so disposed. Amantius appeared to Quintianus in a dream and said "Since you have rashly taken my bones from where they rested in peace, I shall force you from this town and you will go into exile in another land; but nevertheless you will not be deprived of the honour which you enjoy." Not long after this a great trouble arose between the citizens and the bishop; the Goths who were in the town suspected that the bishop wished to submit them to the domination of the Franks, and having taken counsel they decided to put him to the sword.[4] The holy man learnt of this, and got up in the night and left that town with his most faithful servants and came to Clermont. There the holy bishop Eufrasius, who had succeeded Bishop Aprunculus, received him and gave him houses as well as fields and vineyards. He was treated with the greatest respect by that bishop and by the bishop of Lyons. He was indeed a venerable old man and a true servant of God. Then St

---

be suspect in Visigothic eyes.

3. On the church of Saint-Amans in Rodez, see V-T, no. 229. There is a Carolingian *Life of St Amantius*, who appears to have been bishop of Rodez not long before Quintianus himself. It is not impossible that the fifth-century Aquitanian marble sarcophagus in Rodez Cathedral (James 1977 Catalogue A no. 8; illustrated in Cabrol and Leclercq, *Dictionnaire d'Archéologie Chrétienne et de Liturgie* XIV 2458) did indeed belong to the saint, as is traditionally said.

4. In *LH* II 36 it is the citizens of Rodez who suspect him of conspiring with the Franks. In *LH* Gregory makes the events part of the build-up to Clovis' conquest of the Visigothic kingdom of Toulouse in 507, with Quintianus' explusion an example of the Arian persecution of Catholics. But a conspiracy between the bishop of Rodez and the Franks makes no sense before 507, when they are separated by several hundred kilometres, the border between Frank and Visigoth being until then marked roughly by the Loire. *VP* makes it clear that in fact Quintianus was suspected of conspiracy after 507, and indeed after Clovis' death in 511. As we have seen above, n. 2, Rodez was in Frankish hands in 511; shortly afterwards it must have been recaptured by the Visigoths. After that Rodez was on the northern frontiers of the Visigothic kingdom, and the Franks were keen to push further south into the kingdom. A conspiracy at this time seems perfectly plausible. Quintianus flees north into territory that has recently fallen under Frankish control, the Auvergne. It looks as if Gregory in *LH* has deliberately moved the event eight years or so further back, for propaganda purposes. See I.N. Wood, *Avitus of Vienne: Religion and Culture in the Auvergne and the Rhone Valley*, 470-530 (Unpublished D.Phil. thesis, Oxford 1979), 173-4.

Eufrasius died:[5] Apollinaris succeeded him, occupied the see for three months, and then died also.[6] When this was announced to King Theuderic, he ordered that St Quintianus be established bishop in place of Apollinaris, and that all power over the church be given to him, saying "It is for affection for us that he was expelled from his see".[7] Then, when St Quintianus was bishop in this town, a certain Proculus, a man employed in the public finances who had subsequently been ordained priest, did him many injuries: he took from him all power over the goods of the church and left him scarcely enough from which to find his daily sustenance. But Quintianus pleaded with the wiser of the citizens, and all his authority was restored and he was able to protect himself from further attacks. Nevertheless, remembering the injuries which he had received, he spoke as the apostle Paul did after injuries from Alexander, saying "Proculus the publican has done us much ill; the Lord will deal with him according to his deeds."[8] And in the end this did indeed happen.

2. The blessed man was assiduous in prayer, and he loved his people so much that when Theuderic came to besiege the town,[9] the

---

5. Four years after Clovis' death in *LH* III 2: therefore in 515, following the traditional date of 511 for Clovis' death.

6. Apollinaris was the son of the Sidonius Apollinaris mentioned in *VP* III above, who had been bishop of Clermont from c.470 to c.484: they are dealt with in *PLRE* 2 at Apollinaris 3 and Apollinaris 6 respectively. The younger Apollinaris had achieved high position under the Visigothic king Alaric II. In *LH* III 2 Gregory says that the people wanted Quintianus as bishop in 515, but that Alcima and Placidina, the sister and wife of Apollinaris, persuaded Quintianus to cede his place to Apollinaris since he had already been bishop once. The two women sent Apollinaris to King Theuderic, with many presents, and he received the bishopric. There is no hint of these irregularities in *VP*.

7. Another indication that Gregory's version in *LH* II 36 is wrong. Gregory reports Theuderic's words also in *LH* III 2. Although discreet about Apollinaris (see previous note) Gregory is happy to record in *VP* that Quintianus had received his bishopric at the will of the king, hence uncanonically, as Wood 1983 p. 43 notes.

8. Cf. II Timothy 4:14.

9. The attack on the Auvergne and its civitas Clermont was clearly one of the most cataclysmic events in the history of that area: Gregory, an Arvernian himself, refers to it also in *LH* III 11-13, *VSJ* 13 and 23, and *VP* V 2. The event is traditionally dated to 532, but this passage shows very clearly that Quintianus was still bishop: that is, it was 525 or

holy man of God toured the walls all night singing psalms; and so that
the Lord would promptly help the country and the people he prayed
constantly, while fasting and keeping a vigil. Then King Theuderic, at
the very moment when he thought that he would breach the walls of the
town, was softened by the mercy of the Lord and the prayers of this
bishop whom he had thought to send into exile. In fact during the night
he was seized with terror, leapt from his bed and on his own tried to
flee down the main road. He had lost his senses and did not know what
he was doing. His men tried to restrain him, not without trouble,
exhorting him to protect himself with the sign of the cross. Then
Hilping, his duke,[10] came close to the king and said "Listen, glorious
king, to the advice of this humble person. The walls of this town are
very strong, and it is defended by great fortifications. And in order that
your magnificence might recognise this, he has only to consider the
saints, whose churches surround the walls of this town, and the bishop
of this place, who is great in the eyes of God. Do not do what you are
planning; do not do evil to the bishop and do not destroy the town." The
king received this counsel favourably, and forbade any one to be
harmed within eight miles of the town. Nobody doubted that this was
due to the prayers of the holy bishop. Then indeed, when the castle of
Vollore was taken, the priest Proculus fled in vain from the invading
troops to the altar of the church, and was hacked to pieces by the blows
of their swords. And the Lord thus dealt with him according to his
works, as the holy bishop used to repeat.[11]

3.   After this massacre and destruction of the Auvergne,

---

earlier, for his successor Gallus became bishop around 525 (see *VP* VI 5). But *VSJ* 23
says that Gallus was bishop when Theuderic invaded the Auvergne, argue Zöllner (p. 80),
Rouche (pp. 54-7 and esp. p. 491), and Heinzelmann (p. 703 at Theuderic 3), who thus
conclude that Theuderic sent two expeditions into the Auvergne: one at the time of
Quintianus (*LH* III 9-13 and *VP* IV 2-3) and one at the time of Gallus (*VSJ* 23, *VP* VI 2,
3 and 6 [thus Rouche, p. 491 n.13, although those passages do not relate to the invasion]).
Wood 1983, p. 38 n.8 points out that *VSJ* 23 refers to an expedition in Gallus'
adolescentia, not his episcopate, and thus plausibly argues for a single expedition, dated
c.525.

10. Not otherwise mentioned by Gregory: see Selle-Hosbach p. 115.

11. These events are described in *LH* III 13.

Hortensius,[12] one of the senators, who exercised the power of count in the town, had one of the relatives of the saint, a man called Honoratus, unjustly arrested in the street. Quintianus was immediately informed of this. He had his friends ask the count to give him a hearing and to order him freed, but he obtained nothing. Then the blessed old man had himself carried to the place where Honoratus was held, and begged the soldiers to let him go, but they were afraid and did not dare to obey the bishop. "Carry me quickly then to the house of Hortensius," he said (for he was very old and could not walk). His servants carried him to the house of Hortensius, and he shook against it the dust from his shoes,[13] saying "Cursed be this house, cursed also be those who live in it, until eternity, and may it become deserted, so that no-one may live in it." And all the people said "Amen." And he added, "I ask, O Lord, that no-one from this family ever be elevated to the episcopal rank, for it has not listened to its bishop."[14] And as soon as the bishop had retired, all those servants who were then in the house were taken with fever, and after groaning a little they gave up the spirit. After three days, when Hortensius had seen all his servants succumb and feared that he would perish himself, he threw himself in distress at the feet of the saint, asking with tears for his pardon. The saint gave it to him willingly, and sent holy water to the house, and when it had been sprinkled against the walls immediately the illness disappeared, and it was a great miracle: those who had been ill were cured, and those who had not been touched did not succumb to the illness.

4. This holy bishop was very well instructed in ecclesiastical writings, and magnificent in his alms. Indeed, when he heard poor men cry out, he used to say, "Run, I beg you, run to this poor man and give him the food that he needs. Why are you so indifferent? How do you

---

12. For Hortensius see *PLRE* 2 p. 572 (which wrongly gives the name of his son as Ennodius), Selle-Hosbach p. 115 and Heinzelmann p. 627.

13. Cf. Matthew 10:14.

14. This curse is mentioned in *LH*, not in the context of Quintianus' life, but as an explanation of why the priest Eufrasius, son of Evodius ("of senatorial family") did not succeed in winning the bishopric after Cautinus' death despite his heavy bribing: LH IV 35. Archdeacon Avitus was elected instead. Evodius was Hortensius' son, who failed to win the bishopric of Javols: see above *VP* VI 4. On all this see Wood 1983.

know that this is not the very one who had ordained in His Gospel that one should feed Him in the person of the poorest?"[15] He also drove out demons. Having come to the monastery of Cambidobrensis,[16] he found a demoniac there in the midst of horrible convulsions, and he sent priests to lay hands on him. But their exorcisms did not drive out the demon, and the saint of God approached him closely, put his fingers in the man's mouth, and delivered him. The blessed man did many other miracles, and his prayers often obtained what he had asked of the Lord. Thus, one day a great drought desolated the countryside of the Auvergne, and the grass dried up so that there was no pasture for the animals. Then the saint of God piously celebrated the Rogations, which are done before Ascension.[17] The third day, as the procession was approaching the gate of the town, they urged the bishop himself to intone the antiphon that was going to be sung, saying, "Blessed pontiff, if you devoutly intone the antiphon, we trust so much in your sanctity that we believe that the Lord will immediately deign to grant us an abundant rain." The holy bishop prostrated himself on his cloak in the middle of the road, and prayed for a long time in tears. Then he got up, and, as far as his strength allowed him, he intoned the antiphon which they had asked for. Its words were taken from Solomon, as follows: "When the heaven is shut up and there is no rain, because of the sins of the people, yet if they pray towards this place, then hear thou from heaven, and forgive the sin of thy servants, and send rain upon the land which thou hast given unto thy people for an inheritance" (II Chron. 6:26). And when they devoutly began to sing, the humble prayer of the confessor penetrated to the ear of Almighty God, and behold, the sky

---

15. A reference to Matthew 26:40.

16. Location unknown; see above *VP* V 3.

17. The Rogations, days of prayer and fasting, usually involving processions and prayers for good harvest, were instituted by Bishop Mamertus of Vienne (c.470). The "Major Rogation" was on April 25; these are the "Minor Rogations" held on the Monday, Tuesday and Wednesday before the Thursday of Ascension itself (although in some churches they were held on a Wednesday, Thursday and Friday, possibly in the week before or after Ascension: see Beck pp. 104-7). The Council of Orleans in 511 had decreed that the *rogationes, id est laetanias* (from the Greek word also meaning "beseeching": in mod. Engl. "litany") should be celebrated in all churches before Ascension: for three days *servi et ancillae* (male and female slaves) should be allowed to do no work, and all should fast as if in Lent (De Clercq pp. 11-12).

darkened and covered itself with clouds. And before they arrived at the gate of the town, a heavy rain fell upon the whole land, so that they were lost in admiration, and said that it was due to the prayers of his holy man.

5. At length the priest of God grew old, until he no longer had the strength to spit on the ground, and he always had to have a small bowl at his lips to take away the saliva from his mouth. But his eyes were not obscured, nor did his heart abandon the ways of God. He never lost his regard for the poor; he never feared the person of the powerful man; but he always had in everything a holy liberty, and received in his house the mantle of a poor man with as much respect as the toga of an illustrious senator. Then he died perfect in sanctity, and was buried in the basilica of St Stephen, to the left of the altar.[18] Today many people who are sunk in melancholy obtain at his tomb relief from their quartan fever and from their illness.

---

18. He died in 525; his death is celebrated on November 13. The church of St Stephen was built by the wife of Bishop Namatius: "she used to hold in her lap a book from which she would read stories of events which happened long ago, and tell the workmen what she wanted painted on the walls" (Thorpe pp. 101-2): see *LH* II 17 and V-T, no. 82.

V.   About St Portianus, an abbot

How much Almighty God gives to those dedicated to His name, and how generously He rewards them for their faithful service. He promises that He will give them great things in heaven, but often He makes it clear in this world what they will receive in the future. Frequently He renders free those who are in servitude, and those who are free He renders glorious, as the Psalmist said, "He raiseth up the poor out of the dust and lifteth the needy out of the dunghill that he may set him with princes, even with the princes of His people" (Ps. 113:7-8). Of this Hannah, wife of Elkanah, said "They that were full have hired themselves out for bread, and the servants have plenty to eat" (I Sam. 2:5). And on this subject the Virgin Mary, mother of Our Redeemer, said "He hath put down the mighty from their seat and exalted them of low degree" (Luke 1:52). And the Lord Himself in the Gospel said "The first will be last and the last shall be first" (Matthew 20:16). May divine mercy then shine with its love upon the poor, so that the small shall become great and the weak shall become coheirs with the One Son. For He has appointed the poverty of this world to heaven, where the empire of this world cannot reach, so that the poor peasant can go there when he that is dressed in the purple cannot. This is what happened with the blessed abbot Portianus, whom the Lord not only saved from the burden of worldly toil, but whom He also ennobled with great virtues and established in eternal rest after the agitations and afflictions of the world, placing him in the midst of the choirs of angels, from which the prince of this world has been excluded.

1. The blessed Portianus strove always, from the start of his life, to seek the God of Heaven, even among earthly servitude. For he is said to have been the slave of a certain barbarian. He fled several times into a monastery, so that the abbot had to obtain a pardon for him and return him to his master. In the end he fled yet again; his master followed his tracks, and began to insult the abbot, accusing him of enticing his slave away from his service. And when, as was the custom, he rudely pressed the abbot to surrender him the abbot says to Portianus, "What do you want me to do?" And he said, "Give me back, pardoned." And a pardon was obtained, and he was returned, and his master wishes to bring him back to his house. But he becomes so blind

that he can no longer recognise anything. In great pain he calls the
abbot to him and says, "Plead to the Lord on my behalf, I beg you, and
take this slave into His service: perhaps I will then deserve to recover
the light which I have lost." Then the abbot called the blessed Portianus
and said to him, "I beg you, place your hands on the eyes of this man."
And when he refused, the abbot eventually prevailed on him to make
the sign of the cross over the eyes of his master; and immediately the
darkness was dissolved, and the pain appeased, and he was restored to
his original health.

Eventually the blessed Portianus became a cleric, and he was
so famous for his great virtues that when the abbot died he succeeded
him.[1] It is said of him that at the height of the summer, when the heat
of the sun consumed everything and exhausted even the bodies that food
and drink had made the most robust, Portianus, who because of his fasts
had no saliva in his mouth, would chew salt when he was hot, which
brought him some freshness to moisten his dried gums a little. And
although he thereby refreshed his dry palate, nevertheless he brought
greater torment to himself by increasing his thirst. Indeed, as everyone
knows, salt rather excites the ardour of thirst than extinguishes it; but,
by God's grace, this did not happen to him.

At that time Theuderic had entered the Auvergne and was
exterminating and laying waste everything.[2] When he had established
his camp in the meadows of Artonne,[3] the old man hastened to go
before him, as he wished to plead on the people's behalf. And he
entered the camp in the morning, while the king still slept in his tent,
and came to the tent of Sigivald, who was then the king's chief man.[4]
And while he was complaining about the army's occupation, Sigivald
begged him to wash his hands and take wine with him, saying "The
kindness of God will bring me great joy and a great favour today, if you

---

1. The monastery received his name, and the place is now called Saint-Pourçain (arr.
Gannat, dép. Allier). See V-T, no. 265.

2. See note 9 to *VP* IV, above.

3. Vicus Arthonensis, cant. Aigueperse, arr. Riom, dép. Puy-de-Dôme.

4. He was related to King Theuderic, according to *LH* III 13. His sins and the crimes of
his followers are detailed by Gregory in LH III 16, and he is also mentioned at *VSJ* 13-14
and *VP* XII 2 (see below *VP* XII n.2). See Selle-Hosbach pp. 154-6.

enter my tent and deign to say a prayer and then to take some wine."
For he had in fact heard of the sanctity of this man, and that is why he
honoured him, through respect for God. But the saint excused himself
in various ways, saying that it was not possible, because it was not yet
time for a meal, because he ought first to greet the king, and, which was
the most important thing, because he had not yet sung the psalms which
he owed to the Lord. But Sigivald ignored all these excuses, and forced
him to drink; he brought him a full cup and demanded that the saint
take it and bless it. The holy man lifted his right hand to make the sign
of the cross, and immediately the cup split down the middle, and the
wine which was inside spilt onto the ground, together with a huge
serpent. Those who were present were terrified, and threw themselves
at the feet of the saint, touching the marks of his footsteps and kissing
his feet. All admired the power of the old man, and were amazed that
they had been divinely saved from the venom of the serpent. The whole
army ran up to see this miracle, and a great multitude surrounded the
holy man, each person wishing only to touch the fringe of his robe with
his hand, if he were not allowed the honour of kissing it. The king leapt
from his bed and ran to the blessed confessor, and without waiting for
him to say a word, he freed all the captives that he had asked for, and
thereafter he did what the saint requested. And thus, by the grace of
God, Portianus received a double benefit, bringing some from death and
redeeming others from the yoke of captivity. I believe truly, and it has
been confirmed by others, that those saved from this danger were as if
brought back from the dead.

3. I do not want to pass over the way in which the devil tried
to deceive him by various machinations; seeing that he could not harm
him, he began to wage open war. One night, when he had given himself
to sleep, suddenly he awoke and saw his cell all in flames; frightened,
he made for the door. He was not able to open it, and so fell down in
prayer. He made the saving sign of the cross in front and around him,
and suddenly the phantom of flames which he had seen vanished, and
he knew that it had been a trick of the devil. And this was immediately
revealed to the blessed Protasius, who was then a recluse in the

monastery of Cambidobrensis.[5] He hastily sent a monk from there to his brother to exhort him, saying "My dear brother, you must resist the attacks of the devil with courage, and fear nothing from his tricks, but overcome all his attacks by constant prayer and the sign of the cross. He always strives to assault the servants of God by temptations of this kind."

The blessed man grew old, and having accomplished his career of good works he went to the Lord.[6] His tomb is often glorified today by divine miracles. This is all we have learnt of this holy man, and we will not criticise others who have more information about him if they wish to write something in his praise.

---

5. See above *VP* IV. 4 and n.14.

6. His feast day is November 24; the year of his death is presumably not long after the invasion of Theuderic, dated 525 after Wood (see above n.9 to *VP* IV).

VI.   About St Gallus, a bishop

He who is at the summit of worldly nobility always longs for what can satisfy his desires. He rejoices over honours, he is puffed up by attentions, he disturbs the forum with his law-cases, he feeds on plunder, he delights in calumnies, he desires rusty gold, and when he seems to possess a few things he is the more enflamed with a desire to amass many: the more he accumulates the more his thirst grows, for, as Prudentius said, "with amassed gold the hunger for gold increases".[1] Thus it happens that, while he rejoices in the pomps of the world and in his honours, he does not stop to think about the dignities which endure; as long as he possesses things which he wrongly thinks can assuage his passion he does not look towards the things which are not seen. But there are those who, like birds fleeing from a snare and flying up to the skies,[2] have escaped their bonds with the help of a lively spirit and, leaving the terrestrial possessions which they despise, they have turned all their attention towards celestial matters. Such was St Gallus, a man of the Auvergne, whom neither the greatness of his birth nor the elevation of the senatorial order nor his immense riches were able to turn away from the worship of God; neither the affection of his father nor the caresses of his mother nor the love of his nurses nor the obedience of his servants[3] could separate him from the love of God. He regarded all possessions as nothing and disdained them as dung; he consecrated himself to the love and service of God and submitted himself to the rule of a monastery. For he knew that the flames of ardent youth could only be quenched by submission to canonical

---

1. Prudentius, *Hamartigenia* v.257, transl. by H.J. Thomson (vol 1, 1949) as "The Origin of Sin", p. 222. Prudentius, the first great Christian Latin poet, was born in Spain in 348 and died c.410. On this quotation in the MSS of *VP*, see my introduction, p. xxiv.

2. Cf. Psalm 124:7.

3. I have translated *obsecundatio baiolarum* in very general terms, since this seems to fit the sense of the passage. The primary meaning is "porter" or "bearer", and Ian Wood has taken it in the more specialised meaning of "letter-bearer", as found in Jerome or the Theodosian Code. (He too takes the feminine *baiularum* to be an error.) He comments: "Gregory of Tours regarded porters as a vital element in secular society; their obsequiousness could prevent a man from forgetting worldly things": D.Phil. thesis (as n.4 to *VP* IV above), p. 20.

judgement and the severest discipline. He knew also that he had to raise himself from the baseness of the world to more elevated things, and to come by the patience of humility to the glory of the greatest heights. And this indeed is what happened.

1. St Gallus was devoted to God from his childhood; he loved the Lord with all his soul and he held dear in his heart everything that he knew to be dear to God. His father was called Georgius and his mother was Leucadia,[4] of the family of Vettius Epagatus, who suffered martyrdom at Lyons, as Eusebius testifies in his history.[5] They were thus from the principal senatorial families, and there were none better born nor more noble in Gaul. But when his father wanted him to marry the daughter of a noble senator, he went with a young slave to the monastery of Cournon,[6] six miles from the town of Clermont, asking the abbot in all humility to shave the hair of his head. The abbot, seeing the wisdom and breeding of the boy, asked his name, family and country. He replied that he was Gallus, a citizen of the Auvergne, the son of the senator Georgius. When the abbot learnt that he belonged to the first family of the city, he said "My son, you have good intentions, but it is necessary first to tell your father: if your father consents, I will do as you wish."[7] Then the abbot sent messengers to the father to see what he wanted to be done with his son. And he was saddened, and said, "He is my first-born son, and for that reason I wanted him to marry, but if the Lord wishes to call him to His service, His will shall be done rather than mine." And he added, "Do everything that the boy,

---

4. Georgius and Leucadia were the paternal grandparents of Gregory himself: Gregory's father was Florentius, the brother of Gallus. Before Gregory entered the church he was called Georgius Florentinus.

5. Eusebius, *Ecclesiastical History*, V i. Gregory would have used the Latin translation and up-dating by Rufinus. Gregory himself writes about the Lyons martyrs at *GM* 48 and *LH* I 29. At *LH* I 31 Gregory mentions Leocadius, a leading senator and member of Vettius Epagatus' family, and hence one of Gregory's own ancestors.

6. Monasterium Crononense, dép. Puy-de-Dôme. That is six Roman miles, about 10 km. See V-T no. 93.

7. Venantius Fortunatus relates the same episode in his epitaph for Gallus (*Carm.* IV 4): "He fled the embraces of his father, and he left his mother; an abbot was sought as a parent, to rule him as a monk".

by the inspiration of God, asks of you."

2. And when the abbot had heard what the father had said, he
made the boy a cleric. He was perfectly chaste, and when he grew older
he never had any wicked thoughts; he abstained from youthful games;
his voice was always marvellously sweet and agreeable in song; he
always applied himself continually to his studies, delighted in fasting,
and would often abstain from food. The blessed bishop Quintianus came
to the monastery and heard him sing, and did not allow him to stay
there long: he brought him back to the town with him and brought him
up, as a heavenly father, in the sweetness of the spiritual life. When his
father died, and his voice was becoming more and more perfect with
each day, and he was held in great love by the people, King Theuderic
was told about him: he summoned him forthwith and took such an
affection for him that he loved him more than his own son. He was
greatly loved also by the queen, not only because of his beautiful voice
but also because of his chastity.[8] At that time indeed King Theuderic
brought many clerics from Clermont, whom he ordered to serve in the
church at Trier; but he did not allow the blessed Gallus to be separated
from him. Thus it happened that when the king went to Cologne he
brought the boy with him. There was a temple there filled with various
adornments, where the barbarians of the area used to make offerings and
gorge themselves with meat and wine until they vomited; they adored
idols there as if they were gods, and placed there wooden models of
parts of the human body whenever some part of their body was touched
by pain.[9] As soon as St Gallus learned this he hastened to the place
with one other cleric, and having lit a fire he brought it to the temple
and set it alight, while none of the foolish pagans were present. They
saw the smoke of the temple going up into the sky, and looked for the
one who had lit the blaze; they found him and ran after him, their

---

8. The only known queen of Theuderic was the daughter of king Sigismund of the
Burgundians, mentioned in *LH* III 5. Her name was Suavegotho, according to the tenth-
century historian Flodoard of Rheims: see *PLRE* 2 p. 1037.

9. A practice condemned by the late sixth-century synod of Auxerre, c.3. (The acts of
this synod have been translated in Hillgarth 1969 pp. 97-99.) And it has survived in
Mediterranean areas to this day, which suggests that these pagans in Cologne, if they are
barbarians as Gregory says, may be adopting Roman customs.

swords in their hands. He took to his heels, and hid in the royal house. The king learned from the threats of the pagans what had happened, and he pacified them with sweet words, calming their impudent anger. The blessed man used to tell this often, with tears, adding "Woe is me for not having stood my ground, so that I might have ended my life in this cause." He held the office of deacon at that time.

3. At last the blessed bishop Quintianus passed from this life into another, by the will of the Lord. St Gallus was staying at that time in Clermont. The inhabitants of the town went to the dwelling of the priest Impetratus, the uncle of Gallus,[10] bewailing the death of the pontiff and asking who would be worthy to take his place. They discussed this matter for a long time among themselves, and then each went home. After they had gone, St Gallus called one of his clerics, and, being filled by the Holy Spirit, he says, "Why do they grumble? Why do they run about? Why do they debate so? They are wasting their time, for I shall be bishop: the Lord will deign to grant me this honour. As for you, when you hear that I have returned from my audience with the king, take my predecessor's horse, saddle it, meet me, and offer it to me. And if you disdain to listen to me, take care lest you have to repent later." And while he was thus speaking, he was resting on his bed. The cleric was very angry with him: he made many reproaches, he pushed him against the frame of the bed, injuring his side, and then left, still furious. A moment after his departure, the priest Impetratus said to St Gallus, "My son, listen to my counsel. Do not delay, but go straight to the king, and tell him what has happened here. If the Lord inspires him to grant you the bishopric, we shall render great thanks to the Lord. If it happens otherwise, you will at least be recommended to him who will become bishop." So Gallus left, and announced to the king the fate of the blessed Quintianus. At that time also died Aprunculus, bishop of Trier. The clerics of that town assembled, and went to King Theuderic to ask for St Gallus as their bishop. The king said, "Go and search for another, for I have destined the deacon Gallus for another place." So

---

10. The brother of Gallus' mother Leucadia.

they chose and received St Nicetius.[11] As for the clerics of Clermont, they came to find the king, bringing the consent of the people and bearing many gifts. At that time, like a pernicious weed, that custom by which sacred offices were sold by kings and bought by clerics had already started to grow.[12] They learnt then from the king that they would have St Gallus for bishop. He was ordained priest, and then the king commanded him to give a feast for the citizens, at the expense of the public purse, so that they would be able to rejoice in honour of Gallus, their future bishop. This was done. Gallus was fond of saying, indeed, that for his bishopric he had only given one third of a solidus, no more, and he gave that coin to the cook who had prepared the meal.[13] After that the king sent him to Clermont, in the company of two bishops. As for the cleric Viventius, who had wounded him in the side on the bed, he hastened to come before the pontiff, as he had ordered, but not without great embarrassment; and he presented himself

---

11. Nicetius was bishop of Trier by 535, when he attended the Council of Clermont. See *VP* XVII, below.

12. The legislation against the purchase of office in the Gallic church (at Orleans in 533, at Clermont in 535, at Orleans in 549 etc) was clear enough. But its recognition in practice may have been problematical due to the difficulty of distinguishing simony from the customary gifts to kings (and perhaps other dignitaries) upon receipt of high church office. This may explain the apparent discrepancy between the reticence of Gregory in making accusations of simony (this passage in *VP* is the only one which suggests he is worried about widespread simony) and the letters of Pope Gregory the Great (590-604) (see in the English translation by J. Barmby, in the Nicene and Post-Nicene Fathers series, *Epist.* V 53; V 55; IX 106; IX 107, IX 109 etc) which imply it was widespread in Gaul. (Gregory the Great follows usual custom in referring to simony as a "heresy", because of its supposed origins with the proto-heretic Simon Magus.) In a letter to Gregory the Great the Irish abbot Columbanus says that he has heard the confession of Gallic clerics who were worried about the simony they had committed: see G.S.M. Walker's translation in Walker, ed., *Sancti Columbani Opera* (Dublin, 1970), p. 9. "Genuine" election expenses may occasionally have been allowed in the sixth century: see Jones 1964 p. 910.

13. Quite a generous payment, unless the cook has to pay all wages and materials from it. The gold triens or tremissis, a third of a solidus, was the standard hard currency in sixth-century Europe. Some measure of its value might be reached by comparing it with the 4 solidi which could feed a fifth-century Roman soldier for a year, the solidus which a child reputedly cost per year in seventh-century Spain, or an Alexandrian bath attendant in the early seventh century who was "alleged to have kept himself, his wife and two children on a salary of 3 solidi, and moreover to have given freely to beggers' (Jones 1964 p. 448).

before him, not only in his own person, but also with the horse he had been commanded to bring. The bishop and he both went into the bath, and St Gallus gently reproached him for the pain in his side that had been given through the violence of his pride, and so he caused him great shame, since he did not greet him with anger, but only with a spiritual joke. Then Gallus entered the town, where he was welcomed by choirs of singers, and he was consecrated bishop in his own church.[14]

4. When he was in possession of his bishopric, he conducted himself with so much humility and charity that all loved him. He had a superhuman patience, so that, if it is permitted to say such things, he could be compared to Moses for his sufferance of all injuries. Once he was hit on the head by his priest during a meal, but he was so calm that he did not reply with a single sharp word. He bore all that happened to him with patience, declaring that it was the will of God, by Whom he wished to be supported. Once a certain priest call Evodius,[15] who belonged to a senatorial family, attacked him during a gathering of churchmen with many calumnies and insults. The bishop got up and walked around the holy basilicas. Evodius was told of this, and ran rapidly after him, throwing himself at his feet in the middle of the road, asking his pardon and begging that the bishop should not blacken his name in his prayers to the Almighty Judge. The bishop raised him up kindly and excused him generously from all the things he had said, charging him only that he should in future not dare to assail the bishops of the Lord, because he himself would never merit the rank of bishop. This indeed was afterwards confirmed. In fact, having been elected bishop of Javols, and while he was already sitting in his episcopal chair and all was ready for the consecration, suddenly all the people rose against him, so that he was barely able to escape with his life.[16] In the

---

14. This was canonically required, e.g. by Orleans IV, 541, canon 5 (De Clercq p. 133).

15. The son of Hortensius, on whom see above IV 3 and note 12. Evodius had two sons: Count Salustius (*LH* IV 13) and the priest Eufrasius (*LH* IV 35).

16. This must have happened between 535, when Hilarius attended the Council of Clermont as Bishop of Javols, and 541, when Evantius of Javols attended the 4th Council of Orleans. The prophecy of Quintianus (above, IV 3) is fulfilled for the first time; for the second time see *LH* IV 35. On the ecclesiastical politics of Clermont, see Wood 1983.

end he died as a simple priest.

5. In the city of Orleans a great assembly of bishops came together by order of King Childebert, because Bishop Marcus of Orleans had been accused by wicked men and sent into exile.[17] The blessed bishops at this synod recognised that everything which had been alleged against the bishop was without foundation, and he was restored to his see and his town. A deacon called Valentinianus, who is now a priest and a singer,[18] was at that time in the service of St Gallus, and had gone with him. When another bishop was saying Mass, this deacon wanted to sing, from vanity rather than through fear of God. But Gallus prevented him, saying "Stop, my son. When we celebrate the ceremony, by the grace of God, then you may sing. Now the clerics of the celebrant are going to sing." But the deacon insisted that he should sing then and not later. To which the bishop replied, "Do as you please; you will not be able to accomplish what you wish." He did not pay any attention to the pontiff's words, and went and sang in such a disagreeable fashion that everyone laughed at him. Another Sunday, when our bishop was saying Mass, he ordered the deacon to come to him, and said "Now, in the name of the Lord, you may sing as you want." Which he did, with such a fine voice that everyone praised him. O blessed man, to whom was accorded such grace that the voices of men, as well as their souls, were placed under his power, so that when he wished he could prevent them from singing or, if he pleased, allow then to sing.

6. God did other great miracles through him. Julian, who had been a defensor and then became a priest, a man of very sweet character, was taken by a fierce quartan fever.[19] He came to the bed of the holy bishop, and laid down and slept inside the covers for a short time, and woke up quite cured, so completely that he never again suffered from that illness.

---

17. Presumably V Orleans in 549 rather than IV Orleans in 541, as Marcus was present in 541.

18. The word used here is "vocalis": further on Gregory calls him "cantor".

19. Iulianus is shown in *LH* IV 32 as a renowned miracle-worker. "Defensor" means here "ecclesiastical advocate", according to Niermeyer, "defensor" 6.

A great fire broke out one day in the town of Clermont, and when the saint heard of it he entered the church and prayed to God for a long time before the holy altar, weeping. Then he rose up and took the Gospel book, opened it, and went straight towards the fire. Since he had prepared himself against it, it went out as soon as he approached it, so that not a single spark remained from the fire.

In his time too there was a great earthquake, which shook the whole town of Clermont. We do not know what the cause of it was, but we do know that no-one was hurt.

When the epidemic that we call *inguinaria*[20] raged in several regions, and above all ravaged the province of Arles, St Gallus trembled, not so much for himself as for his people. He prayed to the Lord day and night, that while he lived he should not see his people die; and an angel of the Lord appeared to him, his hair and robe shining like snow, and said, "O priest, divine goodness regards you favourably as a supplicant for your people, and, for this reason, do not fear. Your prayer has been heard, and you and your people are going to be deliv-ered from the plague. None in this region shall die of it while you are alive. Do not be afraid now, but after eight years, be afraid." From which it was clear that after this time he would leave this world. He woke up and gave thanks to God for the consolation which He had deigned to give him through this celestial messenger. Then he instituted the prayers called the Rogations, and in the middle of Lent he led a procession, singing psalms, on foot to the church of St Julian the Martyr, which is a distance of about 360 stadia.[21] And while the plague raged

---

20. Bubonic plague. The first great outbreak in the early Middle Ages was in 542: the effects on Constantinople are described in Procopius *Persian Wars* II 22 (transl. H.B. Dewing I (1944), pp. 451-65). It reached Gaul in 543, as this passage shows, since it refers to the prophecy that Gallus would die eight years later, which was to be 551. On the bubonic plague see J-N. Biraben and J. Le Goff, "The plague in the early Middle Ages", in R. Forster and O. Ranum, eds., *The Biology of Man in History* (Baltimore, 1975), 48-80, the translation of an article in *Annales* 24 (1969), pp. 1484-1510. This story is repeated, with slight variations, in *LH* IV 5.

21. As mentioned above (n.15 to *VP* IV), the Rogations were normally after Easter. These Rogations which were instituted by Gallus during Lent seem to be something new. Gregory mentions them also at *LH* IV 5, and says that they, and the procession to Brioude, were imitated by Cautinus of Clermont, during a somewhat different moment of crisis, brought about by the political situation in the town: *LH* IV 13. Brioude is about 65

elsewhere, as we have said, the town of Clermont, by the prayers of St Gallus, was exempt. And it is not, I think, a small favour which this pastor merited, not to have seen his flock ravaged by the plague, since it was protected by the Lord.

7. But let us come to the time when the Lord ordered him to leave the world. He was in bed and ill, and an internal fever ate into his body, so much that he lost all his hair and his beard at the same time. Then, having learnt by a revelation of the Lord that he would die in three days, he brought together the people, and broke bread with them all and gave them communion with a holy and pious will. The third day arrived, which was the Lord's day, and it brought great grief to the people of Clermont. When the sky began to lighten, St Gallus asked what was being sung in church. He was told that it was the Benedicite. And he sang the 50th Psalm, the Benedicite, and then recited the alleluias, thus finishing the whole office of Mattins.[22] Then he said "We wish you farewell, my brothers." And at those words, he stretched out his arms and sent to the Lord that soul which was so intent on heaven. He passed away in his sixty-fifth year, in the twenty-seventh year of his episcopate.[23] Then his body was washed and dressed, and he is carried into the church, to wait until his episcopal colleagues assembled for the burial. He accomplished there a great miracle before the people: the saint of God drew up his right foot on the bier and turned onto his other side so that he faced the altar. While these things were happening the Rogations, which follow the Easter ceremonies, were being celebrated.[24] He lay three days in the church, and psalms were sung all the time in the midst of a great multitude of people. The

---

km from Clermont.

22. Following Krusch, n. on p. 235, this office, which we would now call Lauds, included the singing of the 50th Psalm, the Benedicite, and Psalms 148-150, known as the "alleluiatici" from their first words.

23. It seems that this took place in 551. Thus, if Gregory's figures are correct, Gallus was born in 487 and became bishop in 525, after Quintianus' death. Venantius Fortunatus, *Carm.* IV 4, says that he ruled his church for twenty-five years ("five fives of years") and lived for 60 ("twice thirty"): but it is probable that his figures stem from the demands of his verse rather than superior knowledge.

24. The "Major Rogation": see above, note 15 to c.IV.

bishops arrived on the fourth day, and lifted the body out of the church and carried it to the basilica of St Lawrence for burial.[25] There was such great mourning at the funeral, and so many people, that it cannot be described. The women were in mourning clothes as if their husbands had died; the men had their heads covered as was the custom at their wives' funerals. Even the Jews followed the procession in tears, and held lit lamps.[26] And all the people said, with one voice, "Woe on us, who from this day shall never again merit such a bishop." And as the bishops of the province were, as we have said, far away and had not been able to come promptly, the faithful, after the custom of country people, put turf on the body of the saint so that heat would not cause it to swell. And after the funeral ceremony a woman or rather, as I have discovered by diligent inquiry, a very pure virgin consecrated to God, called Meratina, collected the turf that had been thrown away by the others and put it into her garden. She often watered it, and, the Lord favouring its growth, she made it live. Sick people who took away some grass and made herb tea with it were cured, and even the faithful who said a prayer over it obtained what they wanted. In the end the virgin departed,[27] and the turf was neglected and perished.

Many miracles were also done at the tomb of St Gallus. For those ill with the quartan fever and various other fevers recovered as soon as they had touched the blessed tomb with faith.

The singer Valentinianus, of whom we spoke earlier, who is now priest, found himself taken with quartan fever while he was still a deacon, and was gravely ill for several days. Then it happened that

---

25. One of the churches built by Duke Victorius and mentioned in *LH* II 20, according to Krusch p. 235: on Victorius see also above *VP* III and nn.4 and 5. Buchner (p. 101) also takes this reference to "basicilam sancti Laurenti et sancti Germani Licaniacensis vici" to refer to two distinct churches — presumably St Lawrence in Clermont and St Germanus in Lembron (dép. Puy-de-Dôme). Vieillard-Troiekouroff believes that Victorius founded one church of Saint-Germain-et-Saint-Laurent at Saint-Germain-Lembron (V-T, no. 247) and that Saint-Laurent in Clermont (no. 83) is a separate church, mentioned by Gregory only here at *VP* VII 7.

26. On the large number of Jews in Clermont (or in the Auvergne) see *LH* V 11, which claims that, after Avitus had baptised over five hundred of them, there were still some remaining who refused baptism and moved to Marseilles. On this episode see Brennan 1985 and Goffart 1985.

27. *migrante*, presumably meaning "died".

during a brief recovery he decided to visit the holy places and to pray there, and he came to the tomb of St Gallus and prostrated himself before it, saying, "Remember me, holy and blessed bishop, for it is by you that I was raised, instructed and encouraged; remember your pupil whom you loved with a rare love, and deliver me from the fever which grips me." Having said this, he took some of the herbs which had been strewn around the tomb by the faithful in honour of the saint, and since they were green he put them in his mouth, chewed them with his teeth and swallowed the juice. The day passed without any fever, and in the end he was so restored to health that he had no sort of relapse, such as is commonly called a *fractio*.[28] I learnt this from the mouth of the priest himself. And there is no doubt that He who called forth Lazarus from the tomb draws forth with His power such virtues from the tombs of His servants.

---

28. *fractio*, literally "a breaking".

VII. About St Gregory, bishop of Langres

There are men of outstanding sanctity, raised on earth, whom the palm of a perfect beatitude has lifted straight up to heaven. They are men whom the fetters of true charity bind, or whom the fruits of alms enrich, or whom the flower of chastity adorns, or whom the certain agony of martyrdom crowns; they are men who had such a desire to begin the work of perfect justice that they first offered a spotless body as a tabernacle for the Holy Spirit and thus came to the sublimity of other virtues. They made themselves their own persecutors, destroying the vices in themselves, and they triumph like proven martyrs, having completed the course of their legitimate combat. No-one can do this without the help of God and without being protected by the shield and helmet of the Lord's help; and when someone does it, it is done not for himself but for the glory of the divine name, just as the Apostle said: "He that glorieth, let him glory in the Lord" (I Corinth. 1:31). In that manner the blessed Gregory sought all his glory, when he abased himself from the high power of the senatorial order to such humility that, disdaining all the cares of the world, he consecrated himself to God alone, Whom he preserved in his heart.

1. St Gregory was among the first of senators, and very well educated; he was sought for as count of the city of Autun, and he administered that region for forty years with justice. He was so rigorous and severe in his pursuit of criminals that scarcely one guilty person was able to escape. He had a wife called Armentaria, of senatorial family, whom he only approached, it is said, for the sake of having children. The Lord granted him sons by her, and never, as is so often the case in the ardour of youth, did he lust after another woman.[1]

2. After the death of his wife he turned to the Lord, and was chosen by the people and consecrated bishop of Langres. His abstinence was great, but, so that people would not think that he took pride in it, he used to hide his meagre loaves of barley under the wheaten loaves,

---

1. The sons were Tetricus (Gregory's successor as bishop of Langres); the father of Eufronius (Gregory of Tours' predecessor as bishop of Tours); and the father of Armentaria, mother of Gregory of Tours.

and when he broke wheaten loaves and offered them to people he was able to take a barley loaf for himself without anyone knowing. He did the same with wine; if the cupbearer offered him water, he ordered him to pour it as if it were wine, choosing a glass opaque enough to hide the clarity of the water. He used to fast, to give alms, to pray and to keep vigils, so thoroughly and devoutly that he shone like a new hermit, although in the midst of the world.

He usually lived at the town of Dijon,[2] and, as his house was next to the baptistery where the relics of a great number of saints were kept, he used to rise from his bed in the night, without anyone seeing him, God alone being his witness, to say prayers in the baptistery:[3] its door used to open by divine power, and he could sing psalms there in peace. He did that for a long time, but in the end was seen by a deacon, who followed him at a distance to see what he was doing, without the knowledge of the holy man. And the deacon used to tell how the man of God came to the door of the baptistery, and when he knocked at it with his hand it opened although nobody was there, and when he had entered there was a long silence, but then many voices could be heard singing together for three hours and more. I believe that, since the relics of great saints were there, these saints had revealed themselves to this holy man and sang with him the praises of the Lord. And when he had finished, he went back to his bed and got in it very carefully so that no-one would hear him. And the following day the guardians of the baptistery found it shut and, opening it with the key as usual, they gave the signal, and the man of God rose again for the divine office along with the others.

The first day of his episcopate, when the possessed were confessing him, the priests prayed that he would deign to grant them his blessing. He strenuously refused to do so, lest he incur vainglory, protesting that he was unworthy of being used as a minister of God in

---

2. This preference for the castrum of Dijon was noted by Gregory at *LH* III 19, where he inserts his well-known description of Dijon, the only Merovingian description of a town. When Aprunculus of Langres is threatened by the Burgundians in the 480s he leaves the castrum of Dijon to flee to Clermont (*LH* II 23): clearly even before Gregory of Langres this town was a residence of the bishops. For some recent discussion of the problem, see Wood 1979, pp. 74-5.

3. Vieillard-Troiekouroff (no. 98) has found no other references to the baptistery of Dijon.

the working of miracles. Nevertheless, he could not conceal his power
for long, and he had the possessed come to him, and without touching
them but simply making on them the sign of the cross, he ordered the
demons to leave with a word. Immediately these demons hearing his
command, set free the bodies which their malice had enchained. Even
in the holy man's absence men used the stock which he used to carry
in his hand and expelled demons by raising it and making the sign of
the cross. Likewise if a sick man took something from the bed of St
Gregory, it was an immediate remedy for him. His grand-daughter
Armentaria[4] was seized once in her childhood by a violent quartan
fever, and she was not able to receive any relief from the repeated
attentions of doctors: she was often exhorted by the holy confessor to
apply herself to prayer. Then, one day, she sought the bed of the saint,
and was placed in it, and the fever entirely disappeared, and she never
again suffered from it.

3.   St Gregory went on foot to Langres for the sacred day of
the Epiphany, and was taken by a light fever; as a result he left this
world and went to Christ.[5] His blessed face was so adorned with glory
after his death that it resembled roses. Indeed, the cheeks were red,
while the rest of his body shone as white as a lily, so that one would
have said that he was already prepared for the glory of the future
resurrection.[6] As he was being carried to the town of Dijon, where he
had ordered that he should be buried, those who carried him succumbed
under the weight, while they were to the north of the town and quite
close to it. Not being able to hold up the bier, they put it to the ground,

---

4. Gregory of Tours' mother.

5. His feast-day is January 4, two days before the Epiphany. His son Tetricus was bishop
for 33 years (Venantius Fortunatus, *Carm.* IV 3), and died 572/3: thus Gregory died in
539 or 540.

6.   Brown 1982 p. 227 comments on this passage (although translating it slightly
differently), "We get closer to the aesthetics of the sixth century in Gregory's miracles
than in most other sources. Their taste is rather *art nouveau*. Take Gregory of Langres —
"His blessed face was so filled with glory that it looked like a rose. It was deep rose red,
and the rest of his body was glowing white like a lily." It is a warm echo of tastes which
Virgil had once shared." De Nie 1977 p. 123 points out that roses and lilies were the
flowers associated with Paradise: Fortunatus calls them "eternal flowers": *Carm.* VI 6 2
and VIII 4 11-12.

and then, after they had rested and regained their strength, they picked it up and carried it into the church, which was inside the walls of the town.[7] The bishops arrived on the fifth day, and the body was brought from the church to the basilica of St John. And behold, men in prison began to cry out, addressing the body of the saint, "Have pity on us, most pious lord, so that those whom you did not free while you were on this earth, may obtain their liberty from you now that you are dead and possess the heavenly kingdom. Come to us, we implore you, and have mercy on us." As they said these words, and others like them, the body grew heavy so that it could no longer be held up, and the bearers put the bier to the ground and waited to see what the power of the holy bishop would bring about. As they waited, suddenly the doors of the prison opened, the beam which held the feet of the prisoners broke in the middle, their bonds were loosened and the chains shattered, and they came to the body of the saint with nobody to stop them. Those who carried the bier lifted it again, and the prisoners followed it with the others. Later the judge ordered that they should be free from all punishments.[8]

4. After that the blessed confessor manifested himself by a great number of miracles. A certain religious man said that on the day of the saint's burial, he had seen the heavens open, and indeed there is no doubt that after these angelic acts our saint was admitted to the heavenly assemblies. A certain prisoner was led to Dijon along the same road by which the body of the saint had been carried from Langres. The soldiers marched along, their horses pulling the prisoner after them, until they came to the place where the remains of the blessed confessor had rested. As he passed, the prisoner invoked the name of the blessed bishop, and asked him to deliver him in his mercy. As he made this prayer the bonds fell from his hands. Feeling himself free, he kept quiet, and covered his hands so that the men thought that he was still bound.

---

7. This intramural church was later known as St Stephen: it became a cathedral in 1741 and a corn exchange at the Revolution. See V-T, no. 96.

8. For some comments on these prison miracles see James 1983, pp. 33-6, but above all see František Graus, "Die Gewalt bei den Anfängen des Feudalismus und die 'Gefangenenbefreiungen' der merowingischen Hagiographie", *Jahrbuch für Wirtschaftsgeschichte* (1961), pp. 61-156.

But as soon as they had entered the castrum and reached the forecourt of the church, he ran off, flinging away the rope by which they had dragged him: he was freed with the help of God and by the intercession of the blessed pontiff.

There was also a wonderful miracle by which his body appeared glorious after several years, when his body was moved. The holy pontiff had been buried in a corner of the basilica, in a very narrow place, so that the people could not approach him as their devotion demanded. St Tetricus, his son and successor, realised this, and seeing miracles happen ceaselessly at the tomb, he laid foundations behind that part of the church where the altar was, and built an apse, vaulted with admirable workmanship. He finished the circular wall and then knocked down the straight wall which had terminated the old building, and completed his work by opening an arch in place of this wall. When the work and its decoration were complete he cut in the middle of the floor of this apse a place to receive the body of his blessed father.[9] He convoked for this purpose priests and abbots, who held vigils and prayed that the holy confessor would allow them to translate his remains to the newly prepared place. Then, on the following morning, with choirs singing, they took the sarcophagus in front of the altar and then carried it into the apse built by the holy bishop. But as the burial was carefully being made, suddenly, and as I believe by God's orders, the lid of the sarcophagus came loose at one side, and behold, the blessed face of the confessor could be seen, intact and whole, just as if it belonged to a sleeping person and not a dead man. None of his vestments, which had been placed with him, had rotted in the least. It was not without reason that he was seen to be glorious after his death, since his living flesh had not been corrupted by passions. That integrity of body and heart is truly great which shows

---

9. This is the church of St John: see V-T, no. 100. The description of Tetricus' building works in the basilica of St John is of great interest to architectural historians: it is a rare early description of an alteration made specifically to hold an important tomb. Gregory of Tours' brother, the deacon Peter, was buried here after his murder (*LH* V 5). Gregory clearly wished to write more of Tetricus: all that he wrote in *GC* 105, or all that survives, was the title, "De Tetrico episcopo". Krusch (*MGH SSRM* I p. 816 n. 1) suggested that Gregory died before he could finish it; but in *LH* IV 6 Gregory mentions that he has written about Tetricus "in an earlier book". Thorpe, accepting Krusch, suggests that the earlier book was *VP* VII itself.

grace in this present life and which, in the future, is rewarded with
eternal life: as the Apostle Paul said, "Follow peace with all men, and
holiness, without which no men shall see the Lord" (Hebr. 12:14).

5. A girl was arranging her hair with a comb one Sunday.[10]
The comb, because, I believe, of the injury which she was doing to the
holy day, stuck to her hand, so that its teeth entered her fingers and the
palm of her hand, causing her great pain. She ran weeping and praying
into the basilica of the saints, and fell prostrate at the tomb of St
Gregory, full of confidence in his power. She begged the help of the
blessed confessor for a long time, and the comb came loose from her
hand and she was delivered from her pain. The demoniacs too, when
they confess the name of the saint at his tomb, are often purified. And
several times since his death we have seen these men transfixed to the
wall by the stock which he used to carry in his hand (which we have
already mentioned), just as if they were held there by stakes sharpened
at the end.

6. We know many other deeds of this holy prelate, but for fear
of wearying our readers we have touched on only a few of them. He
died in the thirty-third year of his episcopate, the ninetieth of his life,
this man who has so often been known by manifest miracles.[11]

---

10. For a discussion of "Sunday miracles", see Wood 1979, pp. 62-5.

11. According to Gregory, therefore, he was born in 450/1, and must have become Count
of Autun at a very young — an improbably young? — age, in 466/7, if he was to have
held it for forty years (as above, *VP* VII 1) before becoming bishop of Langres in 506/7.
Venantius Fortunatus confirms the thirty-two-year episcopate in his epitaph for Gregory
of Langres, *Carm.* IV 2: "Coming from an ancient and noble family, he was more noble
still by the merits which raised him to heaven. Once a severe judge, then a holy priest,
those whom he punished as judge he protected and loved as a father. He governed his
flock for thirty-two years ..."

VIII. About St Nicetius, bishop of Lyons

The oracles of Holy Scripture often bear witness to the blessing of divine foreknowledge, which foresees those whom it admits to its kingdom, as we learn from those mystical words from a celestial mouth, saying to Jeremiah, that great prophet, "Before I formed thee in the belly I knew thee, and before thou camest forth out of the womb I sanctified thee" (Jerem. 1:15). And the Lord Himself, who has made both Testaments, when He places on His right hand those whom His happy bounty has covered with the fleece of the Lamb, what does He say to them? "Come ye blessed of my Father, inherit the kingdom prepared for you from the foundation of the world" (Matthew 1:25). And the blessed apostle Paul, that chosen vessel, said "For whom He did foreknow He also did predestine to be conformed to the image of His Son" (Rom. 8:29). Thus He predicted in the case of both Isaac and St John how they should be born, how they would act, their name, their works, their merits. In the same way now, turning to the blessed Nicetius, that ancient compassion of piety which enriches the one who does not merit it, which sanctifies the one who is not born, which disposes and ordains all things even before they have appeared, decided to reveal first to his mother the priestly insignia of grace by which he would be adorned in this world. We possess a small book on his life,[1] whose author I do not know, which tells us much about his many miracles, but which nevertheless does not tell us clearly either about his birth, nor his entry into the religious life, nor the sequence of the miracles which he worked; and so, although we have not found out about all the miracles which the Lord deigned to work through him, either secretly or in public, nevertheless we have decided to tell the things which had not come to the knowledge of the earlier author, although in a more simple style.

1. A man of senatorial rank, called Florentinus, took Artemia

---

1. And we still possess it. It is edited by Krusch, *MGH SSRM* III 518-24. It is a short text — the Life itself is only just over three pages long in the printed edition — and, as Gregory says, it has nothing about Nicetius' family or his early years. Perhaps some of Gregory's information came from the traditions of his own family.

for his wife, and had two children by her.[2] He was sought for the bishop of the city of Geneva; the prince[3] agreed, and Florentinus returned to his house and told his wife all about it. When she heard, she said to him, "I beg you, my sweet husband, do not seek the bishopric of that city, because I bear in my womb a bishop whom I have conceived by you." This wise man heard that, and did no more, recalling what the divine word had once commanded to the father of our faith, the blessed Abraham: "In all that Sarah hath said unto thee, hearken unto her voice" (Gen. 21:12). Finally the moment of labour arrived, and his wife brought forth a child whom she called, at his baptism, Nicetius, as if to announce that he would be the conqueror of the world,[4] and she ordered him to be brought up with the greatest care in the knowledge of ecclesiastical learning. When his father had died, Nicetius, although already a cleric, lived with his mother in the paternal house, working with his hands alongside the servants; for he understood that corporal temptations could only be suppressed by work and hardship.

It happened one day, while he was still in the same house, that there came to his face a bad sore, which grew and became inflamed as time went by, so that the boy was in despair. But his mother continually called on the names of many saints for his cure, in particular the name of the blessed Martin. For two days the child remained on his bed, his eyes closed, offering no words of consolation to his lamenting mother; she, wavering halfway between hope and fear, was already getting things ready for his funeral. On the second day, towards evening, he opened his eyes and said "Where has my mother gone?" She immediately ran in and said "Here I am. What do you want, my son?" And he

---

2. Since Nicetius was the uncle of Armentaria (Gregory's mother) (cf. *LH* V 5), his father Florentinus must have been her grandfather. One of the children mentioned here was thus Armentaria's mother; the other became Duke Gundulf, as we can see from *LH* VI 11. The existence of a member of a Roman senatorial family called "Gundulf" casts doubt on many of the attempts of past generations of historians to work out from the ethnic character of the name the ethnic origin of the person who bore it: cf. James 1988 p. 8.

3. Gundobad, the nephew of the Chilperic mentioned in I 5 above: see *PLRE* 2 pp. 524-5. The election in question is presumably that which finally led to the appointment of Maximus in c.513.

4. The Greek *Niketes* means "conqueror".

said, "Do not fear, mother. The blessed Martin made over me the sign of the cross and ordered me to rise, since I am no longer ill." And, having said that, he got out of bed. Divine virtue doubled the grace of this miracle, for by it the merit of St Martin spread, and a future bishop was delivered from infection. The scar on his face remained as a witness to what had happened.

2. At the age of thirty he was honoured with the dignity of the priesthood, but he did not abstain from the work which he was doing.[5] He continued to work with his hands, with the servants, so that the words of the Apostle might be fulfilled, namely "Work with your hands that you may have to give to him that needeth" (Ephes. 4:28). Above all he busied himself in the task of making sure that all the children born in his house, as soon as they had left the wailings of infancy and had begun to speak, were instructed in reading and taught the psalms, so that when they entered the oratory for the divine office they so could join in the singing that they could perform the antiphons and the prayers, and ensure that devotion might importune the soul. As for chastity, not only did he keep it with the greatest care, but he also always used to recommend the grace to others and taught them to abstain from all polluting contact and impure words.

I remember in my youth, when I was beginning to learn how to read, and was in my eighth year, that he ordered my unworthy self to come to his bed, where he took me in his arms with the sweetness of paternal affection; holding his fingers on the edges of his garment he covered himself with it so well that my body was never touched by his blessed limbs. Consider, I beg you, and note well the precaution of this man of God, who abstained thus from touching a child's body, in which he could not have had the least glimmer of concupiscence nor the least incitement to impurity. And when there might be a real suspicion of impurity, how much more did he avoid any temptation! In fact, as we said, he was so chaste in body and so pure in heart that he never said a dubious word, but always spoke of the things of God. And although he cherished all men by the bond of heavenly charity, he was nevertheless so submissive to his mother that he obeyed her as if he

---

5. For the dates of Nicetius' career, see n.10 below.

were one of the servants.

    3. Sacerdos, bishop of Lyons, fell ill while in Paris.[6] He was so much loved by King Childebert the Elder that the king wished to come to his bedside and visit the sick man. When he had come the bishop said "You know very well, O most pious king, that I have faithfully served you in all necessities and that I have scrupulously executed all that you have commanded me to do. Now that the time of my release has come, I beg you not to let me depart this world in sadness, but that you grant me one favour that I humbly ask of you." And he said, "Ask what you want and you shall obtain it." "I ask," said the bishop, "that the priest Nicetius, my nephew, shall succeed me as bishop of Lyons. For by my own witness he is a lover of chastity, a supporter of the churches, and devoted to almsgiving; both in his deeds and his way of life he does everything that a servant of God should." The king replied, "Let the will of God be done." [And thus with the full consent of the king and the people Nicetius was consecrated bishop of Lyons. He showed himself always a friend of concord][7] and peace. If he was offended by someone he immediately pardoned the offence, or he let it be known by someone else that a pardon should be sought. I saw one day the priest Basil, sent by Nicetius to Count Armentarius, who then governed the city of Lyons with judicial power, to tell him that "Our pontiff has ended by his judgement that law-case, which nevertheless has been opened up again; he warns you that you should not pursue it further".[8] The count was furious at this, and replied to the priest, "Go and tell him that there are many cases heard in his presence

---

6. In *LH* IV 36 Gregory says that this happened after a synod at Paris at which Saffarac had been deposed: he mentions his book about Nicetius at this point. Krusch p. 242 argued that the date was September 552.

7. The brackets indicate a lacuna in all the manuscripts (noted, e.g., in a tenth-century MS in which the scribe had added the words "Here there is much missing"). Some manuscripts contain the words translated between brackets here, but the text appears to be an editor's expansion.

8. An interesting and rare example of conflict between ecclesiastical and secular courts: for some comments, see James 1983, pp. 30-1. Count Armentarius could plausibly be associated with Gregory's own family: the name Armentaria occurs twice in Gregory's connection (and see n.1 to *VP* I).

which will nevertheless be terminated by the judgement of another."
The priest returned and reported simply what he had been told. And St
Nicetius was annoyed with him: "In truth, you shall not receive blessing
from my hand, because you have let me hear words spoken in anger."
He was at that moment reclining at the dinner-table, and I was reclining
next to him on the left, exercising then the office of deacon. He said to
me quietly, "Speak to the priests that they may beseech me on this
man's behalf." I spoke to them, but they were silent, since they did not
understand the holy man's intentions. And seeing this he said to me,
"You must get up yourself and speak in his favour." And I, trembling,
stood up and kissed his holy knees, and spoke up for the priest. He
agreed to my request, and offered his blessing, saying "I beg you, my
dear brothers, not to let useless words which are muttered idly come to
my ears, because it is not suitable for reasonable men to hear the vain
speech of irrational men. You should concentrate your efforts on
confounding by your arguments those who attempt to work against the
interests of the church; as for unreasonable words, not only do I not
wish to admire them, but I do not even wish to hear them." O happy
man, who desired with all his might to avoid giving offence! May those
people hear these things who, if they are offended, do not wish to
pardon, but rather call upon the whole town to share their vengeance,
and do not even fear to have witnesses who by wicked reports say "We
have heard so-and-so saying such-and-such about you". And thus it
happens that the poor of Christ are oppressed by such accusations, and
pity is laid to one side.

4.   One morning St Nicetius got up for Mattins, and after
observing two antiphons he went into the sanctuary,[9] where, as soon as

---

9. *sacrarium* was used by Gregory to mean "sacristy" also, but here presumably means
"sanctuary". The church must be the cathedral: see V-T no. 130 for an excellent
discussion of this important church. It was built by Bishop Patiens c.470, and described
by Sidonius Apollinaris in a letter to Hesperius, *Epist.* II 10, in one of the most detailed
descriptions of a late Roman or early medieval church (and the pillared atrium which
stood in front of it) in Gaul. It is worth quoting, if only as a curiosity, from T. Hodgkin's
translation (*Italy and her Invaders*, II [Oxford, 1892], pp. 329-30) made in imitation of
Sidonius' hendecasyllabic verse:
      See how shines from afar the lofty building
      Which, square-set, nor to left nor right deflected,

he had sat down, a deacon intoned the response. And the bishop was
angry, saying "Let him be quiet, let him be quiet! May the enemy of
justice not be so bold as to sing!" Scarcely had these words been uttered
than the deacon found that his mouth was stopped up, and he was silent.
The holy man ordered him to be called, and said "Have I not said that
you must not enter the church of God? Why have you so rashly
presumed to enter? And why have you dared to sing the sacred chants?"
And all those present were astonished, knowing nothing evil of the
deacon; but then the demon who possessed him began to cry out and
say that the holy man was putting him to great torments. He had indeed
dared to sing in the church; his voice had not been recognised by the
people, although it had been recognised by the holy man, who by his
harsh words condemned not the deacon but rather the demon. The holy
man placed his hands on the deacon, and chased out the demon and
brought him back to his senses.

   5. After having been made known to people by these and other
signs, he passed to Christ in the twenty-second year of his episcopate
and in the sixtieth of his age.[10] While he was being carried to his
burial, a blind man entreated to be placed under the bier, and
immediately he was put there he recovered the sight that he had lost

---

> Looks straight on to the equinoctial sunrise.
> Inly gleams there a light: the golden ceiling
> Glows so fair that the sunbeams love to wander
> Slowly over the sun-like burnished metal.
> Marbles varied in hue, with slabs resplendent,
> Line the vault and the floor, and frame the windows.
> And, in glass on the walls, the green of spring-tide
> Bounds the blue of the lake with winding margent.
> Here a portico, three-arched, fronts the gazer,
> Reared on pillars from Aquitanian quarries.
> There its counterpart stands, an inner portal,
> At the atrium's end, three-arched and stately;
> While within, and around the floor of worship
> Rise the stems of a slender marble forest.

10. The figure of 22 is repeated by Gregory in *LH* IV 36. Krusch believed that he must
have died in his 21st year as bishop. He died on April 2 573. But an inscription (Le Blant
no. 24) has Sacerdos, his predecessor, dying in September 552 (by indiction dating). This
would make Nicetius' death occur in the 21st year of his episcopate.

long before.[11] Thus divine goodness did not long delay in glorifying by miracles the blessed remains of him whose soul it was already receiving among the stars in the midst of angelic choirs.

When the period fixed by Roman law before a dead person's will could be read out in public had come to an end,[12] the testament of this pontiff was brought to the forum where, before the crowds of people, it was opened and read out by the judge. Then a priest of the basilica swelled with rage because the saint had left nothing to that church in which he was buried,[13] and he said "Many people used to say that Nicetius was insensitive; it can now clearly be seen, since he has left nothing to the church in which he was buried." But the following night he appeared in shining robes to the priest, accompanied by two bishops, Justus and Eucherius,[14] to whom he said, "This priest, my very holy brothers, covered me with blasphemies when he said that I had left nothing to this temple in which I rest. He does not realise that I have left there the most precious thing I have, the dust of my body." And they replied, "It is indeed wicked to disparage a servant of God." The holy man turned to the priest and hit him on the throat with his fists and hands, saying "Sinner, you ought to be crushed underfoot; cease your stupid mutterings!" The priest woke up with a swollen throat, which was so painful that he could swallow his saliva only with great difficulty. He had to stay in bed for forty days in considerable pain, but having called on the name of the confessor he was restored to health, and never again dared to prate such words as he had earlier presumed to do.[15]

Bishop Priscus, whom we know to have been a strong oppon-

---

11. A story told also in *GC* 60.

12. The will should be read out between three and five days after death: cf. Paulus, *Sententiae* IV 6.

13. The basilica of the Holy Apostles, later St Nizier, Lyons. See V-T no. 135.

14. Justus, the bishop of Lyons who was present at the Council of Aquileia in 381, and his successor Eucherius, who was present at the Council of Orange in 441. Neither are mentioned by Gregory in any other of his works.

15. A similar story is told about Nicetius in *LH* IV 36, although it concerns a different occasion: two different versions of the same event which come to be recorded as two entirely separate incidents are common enough in hagiography and oral tradition in general.

ent of the holy man, gave to a certain deacon the cape which Nicetius had worn.[16] It was ample, for the man of God was large in body. The hood of the garment was wide, and sewn, as was the custom, with the white bands which priests wear on the shoulder during the Easter festivities. The deacon went everywhere in this garment, and thought little about the use to which he had put it. He kept it on his bed, he wore it in the forum, never thinking that its fringes, if his faith had been firm enough, could have brought health to the sick. Someone said to him, "O deacon, if you knew the power of God, and that of him whose garment you wear, you would use it with more care." He replied, "I tell you in truth that I wear this cape to cover my back — and as the hood is too big for me, I shall make socks out of it!" The wretched man did that straight away, and fell immediately to the vengeance of divine judgement. Indeed, as soon as he had cut the hood, made the socks and put them on his feet, the devil seized him and threw him to the ground. He was then alone in the house, and there was no-one to help the wretched man. A bloody foam came from his mouth, and his feet were stretched towards the hearth; the fire devoured his feet, and the socks as well. This is all I have to say concerning vengeance.

6. Agiulf, our deacon, returned from Rome and brought us the blessed relics of holy men.[17] On his return home he passed by the place where this saint rested, and stopped to say prayers. He entered the building and examined the famous register of the various miracles which had been done there. Then he saw an immense crowd of people near the

---

16. Priscus was Nicetius' successor. Gregory writes of his persecutions of Nicetius' followers and of the sins of Priscus and his wife Susanna at *LH* IV 36. By the thirteenth century both Priscus and his hated rival Nicetius were regarded as saints. Peter Brown comments: "Only readers of Gregory can guess from this one clear example the febrile and insecure accumulation and dispersal of reputation that went to make up what too often strikes the unwary as the marmoreal facade of Gallo-Roman episcopal sanctity. We are far closer than we might think, in the pages of Gregory, to the outright political propaganda associated with the lives of the *Adelsheilige* of later centuries": Brown 1977, repr. 1982 p. 245 (and see also Brown 1982 p. 186).

17. Agiulf was in Rome in 590, and witnessed the inauguration of Gregory I (the Great) as Pope: see *LH* X 1. This visit is also mentioned in *GM* 82. Gregory's life of Nicetius must have been written in 591 or 592, after Agiulf's return and before the death of Guntram in 592, as the king is mentioned as living in *VP* VIII 10.

tomb, buzzing around like a swarm of happy bees around their familiar
hive, some taking from the priest in attendance pieces of wax as holy
objects, others a little dust, and others plucked and went away with a
few threads from the fringe of the tomb-covering, all thus carrying off
for different purposes the same grace of health. The deacon, being full
of faith, could not see this without tears, and he said "If the devotion of
my bishop has made me plough a mass of sea waves with oars in order
to visit the tombs of eastern martyrs and bring back relics, shall I not
take relics from a confessor of my native Gaul, to preserve my own
health and that of those close to me?" And he went forward and
received some herbs from those which the devotion of the people had
placed on the holy tomb:[18] with his hands wrapped in a cloth he took
them from the priest. He brought them carefully back to his house and
immediately the action of miracles justified the faith of the man. For he
made an infusion of those plants with water, and gave it to those who
had fever, and they were cured as soon as they had drunk, and others
were cured later. In telling us this he said that thereby he had already
restored the health of four persons struck down with the same illness.

John, our priest, returned from Marseilles with the merchandise
of his commerce, and fell down to pray at the tomb of the same saint.
Getting up, he saw the broken chains and shattered fetters which had
clasped the necks or calves of criminals, and he was full of admiration.
Even the moment of his contemplation was marked by miracles. Indeed,
when he returned to us he affirmed by an oath that three blind people
had recovered their sight in his presence, and returned home cured. And
when the relics of the saint were being carried with honour around
Geneva in Gaul, amid the singing of hymns, the Lord deigned to allow
so much grace appear there that when they prostrated themselves in
front of the relics the blind recovered their sight and the lame walked
upright, and no-one could deny that the holy confessor was present
when they saw such gifts of cures given to the infirm.

7. A riot occurred at a certain place. The enraged crowd threw
stones and firebrands, and rage gave them no little strength. A man
armed with a sharp sword felled another with a great blow, and a few

---

18. A custom also mentioned at *LH* IV 36.

days later was met by the dead man's brother and was himself slain. When he heard of this the judge of that place had the man put in prison, saying "He is worthy of death, this wicked man who did not wait for the decision of the judge and who by his own will dared to avenge the death of his brother." The prisoner invoked the names of several saints to excite their compassion, and then turned as it were to his own man of God, and said "I have heard tell of you, holy Nicetius, that you are powerful in works of mercy and generous in the freeing of piteous captives. I beg you now to deign to visit me with that excellent kindness by which you have so often shone in the deliverance of others who are in chains." Shortly afterwards, as he slept, the blessed man appeared to him, and said "Who are you, who call the name of Nicetius? And how do you know who he was, since you do not cease to pray to him?" Then the man told him all about his case, and added, "Have pity on me, I beg you, if you are the man of God whom I invoke." The saint said to him, "Rise up, in the name of Christ, and walk free: you will not be restrained by anyone." He woke up, and was full of astonishment at seeing his chains shattered and the beam broken, and immediately, without being stopped by anyone, he went undaunted to the tomb of the saint. Then the judge gave him pardon for the judgement he had been given, he was released and he went home.[19]

8. To these miracles I am pleased to add the one which he did with a lamp which burned near his bed; for the things which the holy man, living in the heavens, now works upon the earth are truly great.[20] The bed, then, on which the saint was accustomed to rest, which had been constructed with the greatest of care by Aetherius, now a bishop, has been made famous by many notable miracles.[21] People adore it with deserved devotion, for those who are taken with fever have only to be placed there and warmth returns and they are cured from their chill. Many other ill people are cured when they are laid out on it. It is

---

19. See *VP* VII n.8.

20. These miracles are also mentioned in *LH* IV 36.

21. Aetherius succeeded Priscus as bishop of Lyons in 586. He organised the cult of Nicetius, and had his Vita written: see above n.1. He was present at the baptism of King Chlothar at Nanterre in 591: *LH* X 28.

covered with a fine cloth, and lamps are kept alight around it permanently. One of them continued to burn for forty days and forty nights, as the guardian assured us. It burned brilliantly without any maintenance, without any new papyrus for the wick,[22] or a single drop of oil; but it remained in its pristine state, bright and shining.

Gallomagnus, bishop of Troyes, came with great devotion to find relics of the saint, and while they were being transported to the singing of psalms their virtue opened the eyes of the blind, and many other sick people obtained cures. Someone brought us a decorated napkin which the holy man had on his head the day of his death. We received it as a gift from heaven. It happened some days later that we were invited to bless a church in the parish of Pernay in the diocese of Tours.[23] I went there and consecrated the altar; I took some threads from this napkin and placed them in the church, and having said the Masses and the prayers I left. Several days later he who had invited us came to find us, and said "Rejoice in the name of the Lord, priest of God, because of the power of the blessed Bishop Nicetius, for you are going to learn of the great miracle which he has worked in the church which you consecrated. There was in our area a blind man, restrained for a long time in the dark night of blindness, to whom appeared in a dream one night a man who said to him 'If you want to be cured, go and prostrate yourself in prayer in front of the altar of the basilica of St Nicetius, and there you will receive your sight.' When he had done this the darkness vanished, and divine power gave him back the light." I have placed more of these relics in the altars of other churches, and there those possessed confessed the saint, and prayer full of faith often obtained its effect.

The servant of Phronimius, bishop of Agde, had been touched

---

22. Papyrus, one of the four exotic imports from the East discussed by H. Pirenne in *Mohammed and Charlemagne* (London, 1938), appears in *LH* V 5 as a normal writing material, and a papyrus volume containing the miracles of Nicetius is mentioned below at *VP* VIII 12; *VP* XX 2 below mentions the preparation of parchment for writing purposes. Papyrus, imported presumably at some expense from Egypt, is not elsewhere mentioned as being used in lamps.

23. *in parochia Paternacense*, dép. Indre-et-Loire. This church was built by a certain Litomer; it possessed the relics of Julian as well as those of Nicetius. See JSJ 50 and V-T no. 204.

with epilepsy, so that he frequently fell to the ground, foaming at the
mouth and tearing at his tongue with his own teeth.[24] He took various
remedies offered by doctors, and for several months did not have any
attacks. But then his sufferings began again, and were even worse than
they had been before. Then his master, seeing the great miracles which
were accomplished at the tomb of the blessed Nicetius, said to him "Go
and fall down in front of the tomb of the saint, and pray for help." He
followed the orders of the bishop, and returned cured, and never had
any relapse of his illness. It was seven years after the cure that the
bishop presented this slave to us.

      9. While the holy man was still alive, a poor man had obtained
from him letters bearing his signature, with which he went to beg for
alms in the houses of pious people. After the saint's death he continued
to use this letter, persuading charitable people to give him quite large
sums of money in memory of the saint. Indeed, everyone who saw the
signature of the saint wanted to give something to the poor man. A
certain Burgundian, who had no respect for the saint, saw this and
began to follow the poor man at a distance. He saw him enter a forest,
and attacked him, and took the letter together with six gold coins;
having kicked him with his feet he left him half-dead. But he, in the
midst of the kicks and other blows, cried, "I beg you, by the living God
and by the virtue of St Nicetius, give me back the letter at least, for if
I lose it I shall have no other means of existence." So the man threw the
letter to the ground, and left. The poor man picked it up and came to
the town. Bishop Phronimius, whom we have just mentioned, was
staying there at the time.[25] The poor man went to find him, and said
"See, a man has beaten me up, robbed me, and taken from me six gold
coins, which I have received by showing this letter." The bishop
reported this to the count, and he, as judge, called the Burgundian to
him, and inquired what he had to say about this. He denied the deed in

---

24. Phronimius was a native of Bourges (*LH* IX 24), who moved to Visigothic
Septimania (for reasons which Gregory admits he does not know) and was made bishop
of Agde by King Liuva (567/8-572/3). When Liuvigild became sole Visigothic king
Phronimius fled to Frankish territory. He attended the Council of Lyons in 585 as a bishop
without a see. In 588 Childebert II made him bishop of Vence.

25. Phronimius is in exile in Guntram's kingdom: this is before 588.

front of everyone, saying, "I have never seen this man, and have taken nothing from him." The bishop looked at the letter, saw the signature of the saint, and turned to the Burgundian, saying "See on this letter the signature, which appears to be that of St Nicetius. If you are innocent, come close and swear, while touching your hand to the words written by the saint himself. We are confident in his power: he will either convict you of this crime on the spot, or, indeed, he will allow you to leave here acquitted." The man advanced without hesitation towards the hands of the bishop, who held the letter open, and as he lifted his own hands to swear the oath, he fell back, his eyes closed, foaming at the mouth, so that one would have thought him dead. After two hours he opened his eyes and said "Woe is me, for I have sinned in taking the property of this poor man." And he went on to tell in detail how he had attacked the man. Then the bishop obtained a pardon for him from the judge, on condition that he returned to the poor man what he had taken, and that he should add two solidi[26] for the blows which he had given him. And so both parties withdrew from the presence of the judge.

10. If one wishes to know how many prisoners were freed by the saint and how many chains and fetters he has broken, one has only to look at the mass of irons which are today in the church, gathered together from such occasions. Recently in the presence of King Guntram, I have heard Syagrius, bishop of Autun,[27] tell the king how one night the holy man appeared to prisoners in seven different cities, delivered them from prison and allowed them to go as free men, and how the judges had not dared to do anything more against them. It is enough for those who have fever, or a chill, or another malady, to take a very small amount of the dust from his tomb and drink it with water, and they will soon be cured. This is without any doubt a benefit coming from Him who said to His saints, "What things soever ye seek in my name, believe that ye shall receive them and ye shall have them" (Mark 11:24).

---

26. For some comments on the value of the solidus, see above n.13 to *VP* VI. The condition about returning what has been stolen and adding two solidi for the blows is very reminiscent of phrases occurring in the Frankish law-codes.

27. Syagrius of Autun subscribed to councils between 567 and 585, and was present at Nanterre in 591 (see above, n.20). See also *VP* VII n.7, in relation to such miracles.

11. There was in the village of Pressigny[28] in the diocese of Tours a recently constructed church, which had no holy relics. As the inhabitants of the place had often asked that we might sanctify it with the remains of some saints, we put in the holy altar the relics of which we have just spoken. And since then the power of Our Lord has often manifested itself in this church through the blessed pontiff. Very recently three women coming from the land of Berry, tormented by demons, were on their way to the basilica of St Martin, and they entered this church. Immediately they clapped their hands together, and cried out that they were tortured by the power of St Nicetius. They threw up out of their mouths I know not what foul substance, mingled with blood, and they were immediately freed from the spirits that had possessed them.

Dado, one of the peasants who had joined the great expedition against St-Bertrand-de-Comminges,[29] and who had several times been in danger of death, made a vow that if he returned home safe and sound he would give in honour of St Nicetius, for the adornment of the same church, some of the goods that he had acquired. Thus he was returning home, and was bringing with him two silver chalices, and again he vowed that he would give them to the church if he arrived home safely. But when he did return he gave only one of them, and in order to excuse the fact that he was keeping the other he gave a Sarmatian cloth to cover the altar of the Lord and its offerings. But the blessed man appeared to him in a dream, and said to him "How long do you hesitate, and pretend to fulfil your vow? Go and give to the church the second chalice which you promised, lest both you and your family perish. As for the cloth, since it is thin, let it not be placed on the gifts of bread and wine on the altar, because it cannot sufficiently cover the mystery of the body and blood of Our Lord." The man was frightened, and hesitated no longer, and promptly fulfilled his vow.

A brother of this man came to the Christmas vigils, and spoke

---

28.   Vicus Prisciniacensim: possibly Petit-Pressigny (Indre-et-Loire) rather than the neighbouring Grand-Pressigny.

29.   *unus ex his pagensibus*, perhaps better "One of those men from the pagus (Mod. Fr. *pays*) of Tours", as Ian Wood has suggested to me. The expedition led to the defeat of the usurper Gundovald after the siege of St-Bertrand-de-Comminges in 585: described in *LH* VII 35-38. On the problems of the definition of *pagus* see Weidemann II, 100-04.

to the priest, saying "Let us keep the vigils together in the church of God, and let us pray devoutly to the power of the blessed Nicetius, so that through his intercession we may pass this year in peace." Hearing this the priest joyfully ordered the signal for vigils to be given. This was done, and the priest came in with the clergy of his church and the rest of the people. But this man, a slave to gluttony, did not hurry to come. The priest sent to him several times, but he only replied "Wait a little. I am coming." What more need I say? The vigils were compl-eted and the morning arrived, and he who had first thought of the celebration was not there. The priest finished the office and angrily hastened to the man, thinking to suspend him from communion. But the man had been corrupted by fever, just as he had been by wine, and he burned with a divine heat. As soon as he saw the priest he begged him with tears to impose a penance on him. The priest rebuked him, and said "It is right that you burn by the power of St Nicetius in whose church you neglected to come to vigils", and in the midst of these words the man died. Then, at the third hour, as the people were reassembling in the church for solemn Mass, the dead man was brought into the church. Nobody could doubt that it had all been accomplished by the power of the holy pontiff. The priest himself told it to us.

We could report many other things that we have known from our own experience or by the recital of persons of trust, but we think it would be too long.

12. Nevertheless, since it is necessary to put a conclusion to this little book, we shall relate an admirable miracle relating to the book which has already been written about his life, which we mentioned above.[30] Divine power flowed from this book, and far from leaving Nicetius without glory, it showed to many people just how glorious he was, in proving the efficacy of the miracles told in it. A deacon of Autun, affected by a painful disease of the eyes, learnt what was done at the shrine of the saint by God, the glorifier of saints. He said to his family, "If I went to his tomb and took some relic of his, or, better still, if I touched the cloth that covers his remains, I should be cured." And as he repeated that and other similar things to his friends, a cleric

---

30. In the Preface to *VP* VIII: see above n.1.

suddenly came to his side and said "You are right to believe that, but
to confirm your opinion of these miracles, here is a papyrus volume
relating to them which will make you believe easily what your ears have
heard." But even before he had tried to read the book he said by divine
inspiration, "I believe that God has the power to work miracles by His
servants." And as he said this he placed the volume over his eyes.
Immediately the pain and the shadows dissipated, and by the virtue of
this volume he recovered his sight, and with so much clarity that he
could read the tales of miracles with his own eyes. It is the one and the
same Lord at work, Who works all things and Who glorifies Himself in
the saints, whom He renders glorious by illustrious miracles. To Him be
the power and the glory for ever and ever. Amen.

IX. About St Patroclus

When the remarkable wisdom of the prophet Moses, following orders from the Lord's mouth itself, set about building a tabernacle conforming to divine dispensation, and had to amass great quantities of materials for this purpose, he found that he did not have enough of what he needed among the stores in his storehouse.[1] So he ordered that the people should know what God had shown him on top of the mountain, so that each could offer some gift to God, according to his means, without being constrained to do so, but voluntarily. Then they offered gifts of gold and silver, of brass and iron, of fine sparkling precious stones, double skeins of fine linen and double lengths of scarlet cloth; some brought rams' skins stained red, and goat-skins.[2] But the doctors of the church have said that all these things are allegorical, and that these various gifts signify various kinds of graces, and they compare the goat-skins with words of praise. And indeed we who are provided with little intelligence, are unskilled in our studies and sinful in deed, cannot offer gold or silver or precious stones or twisted and double skeins; but at least we can lay out goat-skins, that is to say, stories which make known the miracles of the saints and of the friends of God in the holy church, so that those who read may be fired by that enthusiasm by which the saints deservedly climbed to heaven. Since therefore a report has recently come to us concerning the life of the blessed Patroclus, we thought that we should not keep silent but should publish it and, although in poor style, make known what God has accomplished through his servant.

1. The blessed Patroclus, an inhabitant of Berry, was the son of Aetherius.[3] When he was ten years old he was destined to watch

---

1. Exodus 25.

2. Exodus 35:22 ff.

3. Berry is the modern province name derived from Gregory's *Biturigi territurium*, the territory of Bourges. *LH* V 10 says that Patroclus was 80 when he died in 576, so he would have been born around 496. This would mean he was "brought up" by Nunnio during Childebert's rule as king (which began in 511), that is, from the age of 15 at the earliest, and did not decide not to marry until he was in his 40s (see below n.5 for dates of the man who admitted him to the clergy). This does not seem very plausible, and it is

over the sheep, while his brother Antonius was set to study letters. They were in truth not of the highest nobility, but nevertheless they were free. One day they both came at midday to take their meal at their father's house, one returning from school and the other from the fields where he had been guarding the flock. Antonius said to his brother "Sit further from me, you peasant. You herd sheep, while I study letters; the care of such a task ennobles me, while you are made common through your work." When Patroclus heard this he regarded the reproach as a warning from God, and he left his sheep in the field and hastened to the boys' school, born along by his agile mind and a swift pace. There he learnt so readily, thanks to his memory, all that was thought necessary for his age, that he surpassed his brother both in learning and in quickness of thought, assisted in all this by divine power. In the end he was recommended for employment to Nunnio, who was then very close to Childebert, king of Paris.[4] He brought him up with all the care of a great affection, and Patroclus showed himself to be so modest and obedient to all that all loved him with the greatest kindness as if he were a kinsman.

When he returned home after the death of his father he found his mother still alive. She said to him, "Now that your father is dead, my own sweet child, I live without any consolation. I am therefore going to look for a beautiful young girl, free-born, whom you can marry and help to provide some consolation for your mother in her widowhood." But he replied "I shall never marry a worldly bride, but I shall do what my mind thinks best, with God's will." His mother did not understand and asked what he meant. He did not explain, but went to find Arcadius, bishop of Bourges, and begged him to cut off his hair and admit him into the ranks of the clergy.[5] And this the bishop did, by

---

likely that Gregory was exaggerating Patroclus' age at death. Heinzelmann p. 658, commenting on Nunnio, is prepared to accept Gregory.

4. Childebert presumably became king on the death of his father Clovis in 511, and died in 558.

5. Arcadius was bishop of Bourges from 535/8 to 541/9. Arcadius was probably the same Arcadius, the grandson of Sidonius Apollinaris and son of Apollinaris and Placidina (see above *VP* IV n.6), who invited Childebert to take over Clermont in c.525 (see *VP* IV n.9 for this date), and then had to flee to Bourges when Theuderic laid waste the area as a reprisal for this revolt. See *LH* III 9 and 12, and *PLRE* 2 pp. 131-2. For some discussion

God's will, without delay. And shortly afterwards, having become a
deacon, he devoted himself to fasting, delighted in vigils, and exercised
himself in study and in prayer to such an extent that he did not come
with his fellow clerics to eat at the communal table.[6] Learning of this
the archdeacon was very annoyed, and cried, "Either you take your
meals with the other brothers, or you leave us. It is not right that you
neglect to eat with those whose ecclesiastical duties you share."

2. It was not these words which moved the servant of God, for
he already had a burning desire to withdraw into the desert. Thus he left
Bourges, and came to the village of Néris;[7] there he built an oratory
and sanctified it by the relics of St Martin, and he began to instruct
children in the study of letters. The sick came to Patroclus and were
cured, and the possessed were cleansed after having confessed his name.
But he had still not found the solitude which he sought, and his manifest power seemed to him to be bringing him too much publicity. For
an auspice he wrote out little notes, and placed them on the altar. Then
he watched and prayed for three nights, so that the Lord might deign to
reveal clearly to him what He ordered him to do. But the great mercy
of divine goodness had decreed that he would be a hermit, and made
him take the note which hastened his departure for the desert. Thus he
assembled young girls in that place where he was living, and instituted
a monastery of nuns, and then he left, taking with him nothing from all
that he had amassed by his work save a rake and an axe. He entered the
high solitudes of the forests and came to a place called Mediocantus.[8]
There he constructed a cell and spent his time in the work for God
which we have mentioned above. And in that place, since he had restored healthy minds to a great number of possessed people, chasing away

---

of the clerical tonsure, see James 1984.

6. In *LH* V 10 Gregory says that Patroclus never drank wine or cider, but only water
sweetened with honey; he would eat no meat, but mainly bread soaked in water and
sprinkled with salt.

7. Vicus Nereensis: arr. Montluçon, dép. Allier. (The remains of the nunnery may be
those now displayed in a car-park at Néris — pers. comm. Ian Wood.) See V-T no. 179.

8. In 558, for he stayed there 18 years (above, c.3) until his death in 576. Mediocantus
locus later received the name Celle (cant. Commentry, arr. Montluçon, dép. Allier) from
"cella", a small monastic house or cell.

demons by the imposition of hands and the sign of the cross, he was brought a madman, who opened his mouth wide and showed bloodied teeth, because he bit to pieces everything he could reach. He lay in prayer for this man for three days and obtained from the divine mercy of the Almighty that his fury would quieten, and that he would be cleansed from the danger of death; he put his fingers into the man's mouth and chased out the cruel demon who assailed him, restoring him to health. Indeed, the deceits of the iniquitous seducer of mankind had no success with him. Just as he cleansed those who were possessed so he repelled by the virtue of the holy cross the terrible assaults which the author of every crime let loose in secret. During that bubonic plague of which we have spoken,[9] the devil, falsely appearing as St Martin, had wickedly brought to a woman named Leubella offerings which would, he said, save the people. But as soon as they had been shown to the holy man, not only did they vanish by a revelation of the Holy Spirit, but the terrible instigator of this crime appeared to the saint and admitted all his evil deeds. Often, indeed, the devil transfigures himself into an angel of light in order to deceive the innocent;[10] and since he attempted many traps to prevent the saint from climbing to that place from which he himself had fallen, he sent him the thought that he should leave the solitude and return to the world. But when the saint felt the poison dripping into his heart he began to pray, asking that he should never do anything that was not pleasing to God. Then an angel of the Lord appeared to him in a dream and said "If you wish to see the world, here is a column. You have only to climb up there and you will see everything that goes on." And indeed in that dream he had in front of him a column of amazing height, up which he climbed and from which he saw killings, thefts, murders, adulteries, fornications and all the crimes of this world. And when he had descended, he said "I beg you, Lord, not to allow me to return to those abominations which I have long forgotten in Your worship." Then the angel who spoke to him said "Cease then to look for the world, in case you perish with it. Rather go

---

9. Presumably that described in *LH* IV 31, which occurred in 571 and which ravaged the cities of Clermont, Lyons, Bourges, Chalon-sur-Saône and Dijon. It cannot be that outbreak from which the prayers of Gallus had saved Clermont: see above *VP* VI 6 and n.18.

10. Cf. II Corinth. 11:14.

into your oratory, where you may pray to the Lord, and what you find there will be a great consolation for you in your pilgrimage." He entered the oratory, and found a tile on which was the sign of the Lord's cross; recognising this as a divine gift he understood that it would be for him an unshakable defence against all the lures of worldly seduction.

3. After that St Patroclus constructed the monastery of Colombier, five miles from the cell in which he lived in the desert.[11] Assembling monks there he instituted an abbot who would lead the flock of monks so that he himself would have more freedom in the desert. He completed his eighteenth year in the desert. Then he brought the brothers together to announce his own death; he died at a pious old age and in perfect sanctity.[12] After his body had been washed and placed on a bier he was carried to his monastery, where he had, while living, directed that he should be buried. The archpriest of Néris[13] assembled a gang of clerics, planning to take the body of the holy man by force in order to bury it in the village from which the saint had once come. But as he came forward in anger he saw from afar that the cloth which covered the remains of the holy man was of a shining whiteness. He was then, by God's will, so afraid that he immediately repented of the plan that he had conceived so lightly. He joined those who sang the office of the dead and assisted in the funeral with the other brothers who were present at the monastery of Colombier. At the tomb of the saint a blind woman called Prudentia and a young girl from Limoges, also deprived of sight, were found deserving, and received the light as soon as they had kissed the tomb. Maxonidius also, after five years of

---

11. Monasterium Columbariense: cant. Commentry, arr. Montluçon, dép. Allier.

12. See above n.1: his feast-day is November 19.

13. An archipresbyter or archpriest in the fifth century was a senior priest who deputised for a bishop in his liturgical functions (as opposed to an archdeacon, who performed some or all of a bishop's administrative duties). In Gaul however by the sixth century he seems to have been something like the later rural dean, in charge of a number of rural parishes. There is no specific information about his role from the few mentions of archpriests in Merovingian councils (see De Clercq pp. 337-8, and Beck pp. 69-70). Gregory himself only mentions three by name, and three others by title: see Weidemann I pp. 239-40. There is a late sixth- or seventh-century funerary inscription from Brives in the diocese of Poitiers to a "BAUDULFUS ARCEPRB": Cabrol and Leclercq, *Dictionnaire d'archéologie chrétienne et de liturgie*, I 2763.

blindness, came to the holy tomb and received the light. And the possessed, Lupus, Theodulfus, Rucco, Scopilia, Nectariola and Tacihildis, were also cleansed at the tomb of the saint. There were also two girls who came from Limoges, who were anointed with oil that had been blessed by the saint, and were thereby delivered of the evil spirit that assailed them. And in that place every day the Lord, who perpetually glorifies His saints, works miracles in order to confirm the faith of the people.

X.   About St Friardus, a recluse

There are many steps by which one can reach heaven, and it is of them, I think, that David speaks when he says "In whose heart are the steps of them" (Ps. 84:5).[1] These steps of various works are a progression in the worship of God, and no-one can walk this path, as we have seen many times, without being spurred on by the help of God. It is this that the Psalmist means when he says "Except the Lord build the house, they labour in vain that build it" (Ps. 127:1). And this assistance has been promptly obtained, not only by the martyrs but also by all those whom discipline has strengthened in the life of holiness, earnestly seeking what was promised by their thirst of spiritual desire. And indeed, if a desire for martyrdom was kindled in a mind, the martyr sought this assistance in order to conquer; if someone wished to fast he asked it in order to obtain the necessary strength; if someone wished to preserve his body from all attacks against its chastity, he begged for it as a defence; if someone, leaving error, repented and burned with a desire to convert, he implored with tears that he might somehow be supported; and if someone wished to accomplish some good deed, he likewise asked for this help. Thus the steps of this ladder, which is so difficult, high and arduous, are very varied, but by means of this assistance one climbs to a sole God. This is why it is always necessary to ask Him, to seek Him, to invoke Him, so that what the spirit conceives to be good may be accomplished with His help. Thus we ought to say ceaselessly "Our help is in the name of the Lord, who made heaven and earth" (Ps. 124:8). And this is what the holy man of whom we must now speak did; in the midst of different temptations and the crosses of the world he always called upon the protection of heavenly help.

1. There was once on the island of Vindunitta, in the territory

---

1. Slightly altered from the Authorised "In whose hearts are the ways of them", in order to get closer to the Latin version Gregory used.

of the city of Nantes,[2] a man of remarkable sanctity called Friardus, a recluse. For the edification of the church I rejoice to make known a little of his life, because I do not know if it has ever been written down by anyone. From his childhood he was always devoted to God, and very chaste. When he became a man he passed his whole life in praising God, in prayer and in vigils. He took from the earth with his own hands what he needed for his subsistence, and although he excelled others by his hard work he never ceased to pray. And so for his neighbours and for strangers, for such is the way of country people, he was the object of much ridicule. One day he was in a cornfield cutting straw and putting it into bundles along with the other harvesters, and a swarm of those annoying and fierce flies which are commonly called "wasps"[3] came by. They bitterly attacked the harvesters, pricking them with their stings, and surrounding them on all sides, and so the men avoided the place where the nest was. And they mocked the blessed Friardus, saying to him slyly, "May it occur to the blessed man, the religious man, who never ceases to pray, who always makes the sign of the cross on his ears and eyes, who always carries the standard of salvation with him wherever he goes, that he harvest near the nest and tame it with his prayer." The saint took these words as a slur upon divine power, and he fell to the ground in prayer to his Lord. Then he approached the wasps and made the sign of the cross over them, saying "Our help is in the name of the Lord, who made heaven and earth" (Ps. 124:8). As this prayer left his mouth the wasps all hurried to hide themselves inside the hole from which they had come, and Friardus cut the stalks by the nest without harm, in the sight of all the harvesters. This was not done without a miracle, destined for the mockers, for the Lord deigned to strengthen the man who trusted in Him for their confusion.

On another occasion he climbed up a tree for some purpose, and the branch gave way beneath his feet, and he began to fall; as he fell he called upon the holy name of Christ and each time he hit a branch he cried out "Almighty Christ, help me." And when he landed

---

2. Identified by Longnon, p. 312, with a former island on the river Brivet, north of Nantes, now the village of Besne (Loire-Atlantique). The parish church is dedicated to St Friard, and a nearby chapel is dedicated to St Secondel. Sarcophagi traditionally believed to be the burial places of the two saints are in the church. See V-T, no. 32.

3. *quas vulgo vespas vocant.*

on the ground he was not harmed at all; and he always said "our help is in the name of the Lord, who made heaven and earth."[4]

    2. Encouraged by these miracles and others like them he began to reflect and say to himself, "If the cross of Christ and the invocation of His name, and assistance begged from Him, has so much power that it conquers anything difficult on this earth, overcomes dangers, dissipates the horrors of temptation, and renders tedious all things that are reputed to be the delights of this world, what ought I to do in this world but abandon everything that belongs to it and spend my time in the service of Him who, when I invoked His name, delivered me from great dangers?" And he left his small dwelling, forgot his family and his country, and went to find the wilderness, lest by staying in the world mundane activities should be an impediment to his prayers. Together with Abbot Sabaudus, formerly one of King Chlothar's officials, he accepted penance and retired to Vindunitta, an island in the territory of Nantes.[2] They had with them deacon Secundellus. But the abbot withdrew his hand from the Lord's plough and left the island; he returned to his monastery and shortly afterwards perished by the sword for reasons which remain obscure. But St Friardus remained on the island with the deacon Secundellus, and did not leave it. They each had their own cell, far removed from the other. And as they courageously persevered in prayer the Tempter appeared during the night to the deacon Secundellus, in the shape of the Lord,[5] saying "I am Christ, to whom you pray each day. Already you are a saint and I have inscribed your name in the book of life together with my other saints. Leave this island, therefore, and go and work cures among the people." He was deceived by this lie and left the island without saying anything to his companion. And when he put his hands on the sick in the name of Christ they were cured. After a long time he returned to the island and

---

4. He was less fortunate than the recluse Marianus, from the territory of Bourges (*GC* 80) who was found dead at the foot of an apple tree. When a malcontent complained that someone who died while eating apples was hardly fit to be venerated as a saint, his house and farm burnt to the ground. "If someone thinks this happened by chance, let him wonder that the fire harmed none of the surrounding neighbourhoods" (transl. Van Dam, p. 86).

5. The devil appeared to St Martin in the guise of Christ, but Martin saw through him; on the importance of distinguishing between good and evil spirits, see Stancliffe p. 236.

sought out his companion and said to him with vainglory, "I left the island and I did many miracles among the people." Friardus was frightened, and asked him what he meant, and Secundellus told him simply what had happened. The older man was astonished at this story, and sighing and weeping he said "Woe on us, for as far as I understand you have been deceived by the Tempter. Go and do penance, lest his ruses overcome you." Understanding these words and fearing lest he perish, the other threw himself at his feet, begging him with tears to intercede for him before the Lord. "Come," he said, "let us pray together to the Almighty for the salvation of your soul. For the Lord readily pities those who admit their faults, since He has said by His prophet 'I have no pleasure in the death of the wicked, but that the wicked turn from his way and live' (Ezech. 33:11)." But while they prayed the Tempter appeared to the deacon Secundellus in the same guise, saying "Did I not order you to go out to my sheep and cure them, since they are ill and lack a pastor?" And he replied "I found out that you are the Tempter, and I do not believe that you are God, whose appearance you have falsely taken. However, if you are Christ, show me your cross by which you left this earth, and I shall believe in you." And as he did not show him the cross, the deacon made the sign of the cross in the face of the devil, who immediately disappeared in disorder. But he returned with a multitude of demons and attacked the deacon with so much violence that he could hardly escape. At length he withdrew and did not reappear. The deacon afterwards lived in great sanctity, and died when his time had come.

3. The blessed Friardus shone with great miracles. One day he picked up the branch of a tree that had come down in the wind and which, it is said, he himself had grafted, and he made a stock out of it, which he carried in his hand. A long time afterwards he planted this dry stick in the ground and watered it frequently, and it produced leaves and fruits, and after two or three years grew into a tall tree. This was seen as a great miracle by the people, and every day a great crowd came to see the tree, so that the great miracle spread the renown of this remote island far and wide. The saint of God was afraid that he might succumb to the dishonour of vainglory, and he took an axe and cut down the tree. Another time the saint saw that a tree all covered in blossom had been thrown to the ground by the violence of a furious wind. He was touched

with compassion, and began to pray, saying "I beg you, Lord, that the fruits of this tree should not perish, since it is by Your will that it has produced the flowers with which it is adorned. May it on the contrary live again and grow and achieve the maturity of its fruit." And having spoken he took an axe and separated the trunk from its roots. Then he sharpened the trunk like a stake and planted it in the ground. Although planted without roots the tree recovered its former aspect, and the withered flowers took again their earlier freshness, and that same year the tree bore fruits for its cultivator. This miracle makes me believe that by the mercy of God this saint could well raise men from death by his prayers just as he obtained that withered trees should burst into leaf with renewed greenness.

4. The saint had several times predicted to his brothers the time of his death. One day he was attacked by a fever and he says to them "Go to Bishop Felix and tell him of my departure, saying: 'Your brother Friardus says: Behold, the course of my life has ended, I am leaving this world, and so that you may be more certain of my words, know that I shall leave next Sunday and go to that rest which God, the eternal king, has promised to me. Come then, I pray you, that I may see you before I die.'" But Felix could not come, retained by I know not what circumstances,[6] and he sent the message: "I beg you, if it is possible, wait for me a little while until I have been freed from the burden of official duties and I may come to you." The messengers brought these words to the saint when he was already in his bed, and he cried, "Let us then get up and wait for our brother!" Man of ineffable sanctity! Although he was in haste to come to his end and be with Christ, yet he did not forget friendship, and he obtained from God that he might have a longer stay in this world so that he could see his brother with spiritual respect. And I do not believe that Felix's merit was small, for whose coming the Lord deigned to extend the life of this saint. Having heard of the delay from the messengers, Friardus immed-

---

6. An odd comment, given the explanation Gregory then goes on to give. One wonders if this slightly odd, if not comic, life of Friardus, the only Nantais saint in Gregory's works, and the most rustic of them all, was not influenced by Gregory's own antipathy towards his episcopal colleague Felix (on which see W.C. McDermott, "Felix of Nantes: a Merovingian bishop", *Traditio*, 31 (1975), 1-24).

iately felt the fever leave him, and he got up from his bed, quite healthy. A long time afterwards the bishop arrived. The saint, who had just been seized by his fever again, greets him on his entry and kissed him, saying "You are making me wait a long time on that path which I must take, O holy bishop." They kept the vigils together all night, which was that of Sunday, and immediately the morning came he gave up the spirit.[7] Straightway the whole cell shook, and was filled with a sweet odour; from which it is certain that angelic power was there, which perfumed his cell with divine odours in order to mark the saint's merit.[8] His glorious body was washed and enclosed in its tomb by the bishop, and his soul was received in heaven by Christ, leaving to the inhabitants of this earth the example of his virtues.

---

7. Gregory tells us (*LH* IV 37) that Friardus died at exactly the same time as St Nicetius, that is, in 573.

8. *LH* IV 37 does not mention the odour, but says that the whole cell shook at his death, showing thereby that an angel had come.

XI.   About St Caluppa, a recluse

The poverty of this world always unlocks the celestial palace, and it not only prepares those who choose it for the heavens but also renders those who are gloried by miracles famous in this world. While the chains worn in this terrestrial prison open the door to paradise, the soul which finds itself joining the choirs of angels rejoices in eternal rest. Thus we do not wish to pass over in silence what we know about the blessed recluse Caluppa.

1. This man from the beginning of his life[1] always sought the blessing of obedience to the church, and he found it, and retired to the monastery of Méallat in the Auvergne,[2] and there lived in great humility towards his brothers. He kept such an excessive abstinence that he was too weakened by his fasting to accomplish the daily work done by the other brothers. As is the custom of monks, they complained bitterly, particularly the prior, who said to him "He who does not choose to work does not deserve to eat." Thus, harassed all the time by reproaches of this sort, he set his eyes on a valley not far from the monastery, in the midst of which was a great natural crag, some five hundred feet high and quite isolated from the surrounding mountains. This valley was watered by a stream, which gently bathed the foot of the crag. The holy man entered a rocky cleft in the crag, which had formerly served as a refuge in times of invasion, and, cutting away some rock, he established his dwelling there. It could only be reached by a very difficult path, for that place is so difficult of access that even wild beasts can only get there with some trouble. He put together a small oratory, where, as he used to tell us with tears, snakes often used to fall on his head while praying, and twist around his neck, filling him with terror. And since the devil often takes the shape of the wily serpent, there can be no doubt that it was he who attempted this attack. But as the saint stayed quite still and was not moved by the attacks of

---

1. From *LH* V 9 we learn that he died in 576; as he was in his 50th year (*VP* XI 3), he was born c.526.

2. Monasterium Meletinse: probably Méallat, arr. Mauriac, dép. Cantal, despite the fact that no memory of the saint survived there. The valley of the Marlhoux corresponds to Gregory's description: see Fournier pp. 413-4 and V-T no. 157.

small snakes, one day two enormous dragons came towards him, and stopped some distance away. One of them, stronger than the other, and, I believe the very chief of every temptation, puffed out its chest and raised its mouth to the height of the holy man's mouth, as if it wanted to speak to him. The saint was so terrified that he stayed as rigid as bronze; he was not able to move a limb, not even to lift his hand to make the sign of the cross. And after they had both stayed silent like this for a long time, it came to the saint's mind that he could say the Lord's prayer to himself, even if he could not move his lips to say it aloud. While he spoke in silence, his limbs, which had been enchained by the arts of his enemy, began to relax little by little, and when he felt his right hand free he made the sign of the cross on his face, and then turned to the hydra and made the sign of the cross over it, saying "Are you not the one who forced the first man out of paradise, who reddened the hand of a brother with the blood of his own brother, who roused Pharaoh to persecute the people of God and who finally incited the Jewish people to pursue the Lord with a blind fury? Go far away from the servants of God, by whom you have many times been defeated and covered in confusion; for you have been chased as Cain and supplanted in the person of Esau; you have been toppled as Goliath; you have been hanged as the traitor Judas; and in the same cross of divine power you have been defeated and conquered, with your powers and your dominations. Hide your head, then, enemy of God, and humiliate yourself under the sign of the divine cross, because you have nothing in common with the servants of God, whose inheritance is the kingdom of Christ." The saint said these things and others like them, and with each phrase he made the sign of the cross. The dragon was conquered by the power of that standard, and went to hide himself in humiliation. But while these things were happening the other serpent entwined itself insidiously around his legs and feet. The holy hermit saw this serpent twisted around his feet, and prayed, and ordered him to leave, saying "Get thee behind me, Satan! You are not able to harm me, in the name of Christ my Lord." It retired as far as the entrance to the cave, letting out a formidable noise from its rear end as it did so, and filling the little cell with such a stink that it could be none other than the devil himself. And since then neither serpent nor dragon ever appeared to the saint.

2.   He was assiduous in the work of God, and never did

anything but read or pray, and even when he took a little food he still went on praying. He fished occasionally in the river, but seldom, and when he did so the fish came straight to him, by the will of God. As for bread, he only received it from the monastery; if some devout person brought him loaves or wine he gave it all for the nourishment of the poor, or to those who asked to receive from him either the saving sign of the cross or the relief of their sufferings; that is to say, to those to whom he had given health by his prayers he also gave food to eat, recalling what the Lord said in the Gospel of the crowds whom He had cured from various illnesses: "I will not send them away fasting, lest they faint in the way" (Matthew 15:32). And I do not think that I should conceal the benefits which divine goodness gave to him in that place. Since water had to be brought to him from the bottom of the valley, about ten stadia away,[3] he begged the Lord to make a spring appear in the very cell in which he lived. And that celestial power which had once caused water to come from a rock for thirsting peoples did not fail him here; instantly at his prayer a spring came forth from the rock and fell to the ground and formed rivulets on all sides. The saint was delighted with this gift from heaven, and dug into the rock a small basin which served him as a cistern and which held nearly two condia. In this he preserved the water which had been divinely given to him, of which he received each day only enough for him and for the boy who had been charged to serve him.

3. We met this man in this place, when we were in the company of the blessed Bishop Avitus.[4] Everything we have related we heard from the saint himself, and other things we have seen with our own eyes. He was ordained deacon and priest by the pontiff we have just named. He gave many salutary remedies to those who were assailed by different illnesses. Nevertheless he never left his cell to show himself to anyone, but used to stretch his hand out of a small window to give his blessing with the sign of the cross; and if someone visited him he would approach this window and offer prayer or conversation. Finally

---

3. Just under 3 km.

4. Bishop of Clermont, c.572-94, Gregory's teacher (see above, *VP* II, Preface and *VP* II n.1).

he completed the course of his life in this religious way, in the fiftieth year of his age, if I am not deceived, and then went to the Lord.[5]

---

5. See n.1 above. His feast-day is March 5.

XII.   About St Aemilianus, a hermit, and St Brachio, an abbot

The Holy Spirit teaches us by the mouth of the Psalmist how much heavenly discipline grants to those who keep it, and how it has to be imposed upon those who do not observe it: "Receive discipline, lest the Lord be angry and ye perish from the right way" (Ps. 2:12). And of the good man Solomon said that "the chastisement of our peace was upon him" (Isaiah 53:5). This discipline establishes fear of the Lord; fear of the Lord is the beginning of wisdom; wisdom teaches the love of God; love of God raises man above the things of the earth; it summons him to heaven and places him in paradise, where the souls of the blessed take new wine from the vine of life and feast in the kingdom of God. It was necessary then that men should desire to drink the mystery of this wine, so that they might be able to approach that most pleasant place of delights. The vines that we see now extending their branches, with shoots sprouting, tendrils entwining and grapes hanging, have so many charms for the eye, not only because of the abundant fruits they carry but also for the shade which protects us when we are burnt by the rays of the sun. But we know that when the fruit has been picked, in due season, the leaves drop off, as if withered. We ought the more to desire those things which never come to an end and never wither in the heat of temptation, where even after hope has been lost the thing hoped for can be attained and enjoyed. Many have not only wished to abandon all their riches, but have even retired bravely into the deserts and wild places, in order to quench the thirst of their aspiration for the solitary and remote life with the help of prayer and with the tears of repentance. It is clear that this was the case with the blessed Aemilianus, who lived in our own days the life of the hermits.

1. Aemilianus left his family and his property and went to find solitude in the desert, in the most remote places of the forest of Pionsat in the Auvergne.[1] Clearing the trees he made a small field, which he

---

1. *Silvae Ponticiacenses*: probably Pionsat, arr. Riom, dép. Puy-de-Dôme. The patron of the church at Pionsat is St Bravy, probably Brachio, although the feast-day of Bravy is 9 February and that of Brachio is 15 September: see V-T, no. 206. This discrepancy is probably explained by one date being that of the translation of the relics mentioned at the end of *VP* XII 3.

cultivated with a hoe and which furnished for him all the necessities of life. He also had a small garden which he watered with rainwater and from which he gathered vegetables, which he ate without any seasoning. He had no other consolations except the help of God, for there were no other inhabitants there except the beasts and the birds, who gathered around him every day as around a servant of God. He gave all his time to fasting and to prayer, and for this reason no worldly cares distracted him, because he sought God alone.

2.   There was then in the town of Clermont a man endowed with considerable power, called Sigivald,[2] who had in his service a young man called Brachio, which means in their language "bear-cub".[3] The man of whom I have just spoken charged the other to hunt boars. Accompanied by a great number of dogs Brachio hunted through the forest, and if he took something he brought it to his master. One day, as he was pursuing a boar of enormous size with his pack, the boar came within the boundary which was around the saint's cell. The pack of dogs followed it, barking, and came as far as the entrance to the forecourt, and immediately they stopped short in their tracks, for it was not permitted to them to enter after the boar. Seeing this Brachio recognised with astonishment that there was something divine at work. He went towards the cell, and saw there the boar standing fearlessly in front of the door. The old man came to greet Brachio, kissed him, invited him to sit down, and when they had sat he said to him "I see that you are dressed very elegantly, my dear son, and that you follow those things that prepare the soul for damnation rather than for salvation. I beg you to abandon your worldly master and follow the true God, the creator of heaven and earth, who governs all by His will, who submits everything to His rule, and by whose almighty power, as you see, this beast stands unafraid. May the power of your master, which is

---

2.   Theuderic appointed his relative Sigivald to control Clermont after its capture in 525 (see above n.9 to *VP* IV for this date). At *LH* III 16 Gregory describes Sigivald's various crimes, and refers to a miracle by which he repented, described in *VSJ* 14. Gregory also refers to him at *VP* V 2 above; see Heinzelmann p. 695.

3.   At *LH* V 12 Gregory says that Brachio was a Thuringian by birth. Cf. German "Bracke", which means, however "hound" or "pointer". It may be that Gregory gets it wrong, on one of the very few occasions on which he tries to translate a Germanic word.

nothing, not make you vain and full of pride. For the Apostle Paul has said 'He that glorieth, let him glory in the Lord' (I Corinth. 1:31). And elsewhere, 'If I pleased men, I should not be the servant of Christ' (Galat. 1:10). Make yourself the subject of Him who says 'Come unto me all ye that labour and are heavy laden, and I will give you rest' (Matthew 11:28). For He is the Lord, whose burden is light, whose yoke is gentle, whose worship both offers rewards and bestows eternal life. Such are indeed His words: 'If someone renounces all that he possesses, he shall receive an hundredfold, and shall inherit everlasting life' (Matthew 19:29)." While the old man was talking vigorously in this fashion, the boar withdrew safely into the forest. The young man left the saint filled with a great admiration, having seen the boar which he had begun by hunting become, despite its natural ferocity, as gentle as a lamb in the presence of the old man. So he reflected on what he had been told, and asked himself what he should do, whether he should leave the world or continue to serve it. He was touched by divine goodness, and I believe by the prayer of the holy Aemilianus, and he started to look for some secret way of joining the ranks of the clergy: he did not dare do so publicly because of his worldly master. And although he was still a layman he used to rise from his bed two or three times in the night and fall down to pray to God. But he did not know what to sing because he had not been instructed in letters. Then, having often seen in the oratory letters written above the images of the apostles and other saints,[4] he copied these into a book; and as clerics and abbots would frequently come and visit his master he used to seek out the youngest of them and ask them the names of the letters, and then he began to understand them. And, inspired by the Lord, he knew how to read and write before even knowing all his letters. When Sigivald died[5]

---

4. *super iconicas*, a word also used by Gregory at *GM* 21. *GM* 21 and 22 are the earliest known stories of miracle-working icons, as Robert Markus pointed out in "The cult of icons in sixth-century Gaul", *Jnl. of Theological Studies*, 29 (1978), 151-7, now reprinted with an additional note in Markus, *From Augustine to Gregory the Great: History and Christianity in Late Antiquity* (London, 1983). See also J. Hubert, "La décoration peinte des sanctuaires de la Gaule d'après un épisode de la vie de l'abbé Brachio raconté par Grégoire de Tours", *Bull. Soc. Antiq. France* (1942), 91-5.

5. *LH* III 23: "At that time Theuderic put his relative Sigivald to the sword." This happened shortly before Theuderic's death in 534.

he hastened to the old man, and having spent two or three years with him, he learnt the psalter by heart. Nevertheless his brother, seeing that he did not wish to marry, often thought of killing him. Later, some monks came to join the old man and himself.

3. At length the blessed Aemilianus completed the measure of the days allotted for his life; he died in about the ninetieth year of his age, and left Brachio as his successor. The latter founded a monastery and obtained from Ranichild, daughter of the same Sigivald, several pieces of land which he left to the community. They were woods belonging to the villa of Vensat.[6] Then Brachio left the community and came to Tours, where he built oratories and founded two monasteries.

One day travellers arrived carrying the relics of saints, which they placed on the altar of St Martin's church in Tours, as they planned to leave the following day. Abbot Brachio was keeping a vigil in the church, and saw around midnight a great globe of fire, which left the relics and rose with a great light towards the roof of the church. There was without doubt something divine about this, but it was seen only by him and not by those with him.[7] After that he returned to the Auvergne, to his first monastery; he stayed there for five years and then returned to Tours; he established abbots in the monasteries he had founded and then went back to the Auvergne. And while he was living in his former cell he was charged to re-establish the rule in the monastery of Menat,[8] which had been relaxed through the negligence of the abbot, so that by his care the community might live according to the canons. He himself lived a most pure life, and strenuously tried to make others keep a

---

6. *Domus Vindiciacensis*, possibly St-Saturnin-de-Vensat, arr. Riom, dép. Puy-de-Dôme. But, partly on grounds of its distance of 40 km from Pionsat, Vieillard-Troiekouroff (at no. 369), prefers to regard it as unidentified.

7. A miracle mentioned in *GC* 38, where Gregory writes "as I wrote in the book of his life" (i.e. *VP* XII). Here, however, Gregory says that "not many" saw the miracle. In GC 20 Gregory mentions another globe of fire, which was seen by many in the oratory which he had built in Tours that contained the relics of Saturninus, Martin and Illidius: see above *VP* II 3. For Gregory's views on the witnessing of miracles, cf. *GM* 85, where he recounts a miracle and adds, "I confess I was present then at the festival, but I was not wortthy to see this."

8. *Monasterium Manatinse*: arr. Riom, dép. Puy-de-Dôme. The modern French place-name appears to be Menat, not Ménat as in V-T.

chaste life too. His conversation was gentle, his manner affable, but he was so severe against those who broke the rule that sometimes he was thought to be cruel. He had attained perfection as far as fasting, vigils and charity were concerned. And when the time of his death approached, he had a dream, as he himself told the blessed bishop Avitus, in which he was taken up to heaven into the presence of the Lord. There he saw the seraphim who shadowed the divine majesty with their outstretched wings;[9] the prophet Isaiah held out a book and prophesied in a great voice. And while he was contemplating all this with astonishment, he awoke. He examined the dream carefully and saw that God thereby announced the end of his life. He says to the abbot whom he had appointed in the first monastery: "The place near the river, where I had thought of building an oratory, is very pleasant. I beg you to carry out my wish, which is that my bones should be laid there." When he died he was buried in the oratory of his former cell.[10] But the abbot wished to carry out the wish of the saint, and with God's permission he put together in that place lime which had been long prepared, and foundations of the size he wanted. Then, the work being finished, he opened the grave of Abbot Brachio, whose body remained intact as if he had died the day before; and thus, two years after his death, he was transferred to that place with great joy by the congregation of monks that he himself had instructed.

---

9. Cf. Isaiah 6:2.

10. *LH* V 12: "After these things Abbot Brachio of the monastery of Menat died." This appears to have been in 576.

XIII.   About St Lupicinus

The athletes of Christ and the conquerors of the world have desired to lose this fleeting life and tp proceed to that life of perpetual joy, where there is no pain, which has no end, whose light will never go out and whose serenity will never be obscured by any cloud. And for this reason they have always counted the trials and tribulations of this present life as nothing, knowing well that for the small troubles which they have suffered they will later obtain great joys. This is why whoever takes part in this fight is not frightened by any fear, turned away by any troubles or discouraged by any pain, if only he may merit the enjoyment of eternal happiness with the chosen of God. This we know to have been done many times by the holy men whose life is now being written or read.

1.   A certain Lupicinus, a person of great holiness and very strong in the works of the Lord, had as a young man been accustomed to asking for alms at the houses of pious people; he gave all that he could acquire thus to others like him. When he reached the middle of his life he came to vicus Berberensis, which is now called Lipidiacum.[1] There he found old walls, in which he enclosed himself, withdrawing from the sight of men. He received through a little window small quantities of bread and water, which sometimes used to last him for three days, even though he was given very little. He received the water by means of a small channel; the window was covered up by a cloth. And both openings were so hidden that it was not possible for anyone to see the blessed face of the hermit. And while he was there he delighted in the singing of psalms in praise of God, day and night. But he sought for further means of afflicting his poor body, for he recalled the words of the Apostle that "the sufferings of this present time are not worthy to be compared with the glory that shall be revealed in us" (Romans 8:18). And he wore on his neck, all through the day, while he sang the praises of God in his cell, a large stone, which two men could hardly lift. And in the night, to mortify himself further, he fixed on the

---

1. Uncertain location. G. Fournier pp. 173-5 believes it to be Lubié, although that had already been rejected by Longnon in favour of Dompierre-sur-Bèbre. See V-T, no. 373: she inclines towards Longnon's suggestion.

end of his staff two thorns, whose points were turned outwards; he placed this under his chin lest he should fall asleep. Towards the end of his life his chest was so crushed by the weight of the stone he wore that blood began to come from his mouth; he used to spit this out against the walls. Trustworthy people who stealthily approached his cell at night have said that they could hear the voices of many people singing psalms. Many sick people and those tormented by fever or sores have been cured simply by touching his hand, or by receiving his blessing with the saving sign of the cross.

2. When he had become stooped with age he called his servant and said to him "The time to hide things is past; now the time to speak has come. Know then that in three days I shall be delivered from this world. Now call all the faithful, my brothers and my sons, to come and visit us. I wish to bid them farewell." At daybreak on the third day his brothers came in a crowd. The door which had been closed now opened and all present entered, and he greeted them all and kissed them. He prayed to the Lord, saying "I offer thee thanks, O Lord Jesus Christ, who has commanded my deliverance from all the toils of this world. You have deigned to cherish me in this world in such a way that the author of every crime could find nothing of himself in me." And turning towards the people he says "I beg you, well-beloved people, 'Magnify the Lord with me, and let us exalt His name together' (Ps. 34:3). It is He who has lifted me from the mud, who has rescued me from the works of darkness and who allowed me to share in the joy of His friends. It is He who has sent His angel to recall me from this worldly dwelling, and who has promised to lead me to eternal rest, so that having become a colleague of His friends I should be worthy to be admitted into His kingdom." O blessed man, who has merited to be consoled in this body, to the point of knowing what he would enjoy in heaven before he left this world! He deserved to obtain here below from the divine power what David asked for so often: "Lord, make me to know mine end, and the measure of my days what it is; that I may know how frail I am" (Ps. 39:4). Then, lying on the ground, he

surrendered to the Lord that spirit which yearned for heaven.[2] Then all fall down and weep. Some kiss his feet; others take away some fragment of his garment; others collect from the walls the blessed blood that he had spat out. And indeed scuffles break out among them, for each thought himself wretched if he left without having some relics of the holy man to take with him. The wall today still witnesses to what we have just said, for it has as many little holes as it had merited drops of spittle from the mouth of the blessed man. The channel from which the holy man drew the water he needed is another witness; in kissing it with faith one can drink health from it. I have indeed myself seen many who had scraped from the wall the spit which had come from that sanctified mouth, who have had the honour of relief from several illnesses.

3. When the saint had died a respectable woman washed the body and dressed it in suitable clothes, and then wanted to take it to the village of Trézelle.[3] But the people of Lipidiacum opposed her, saying "It is our ground which nourished him, so the remains of his body belong to us." But the woman replied "If you base your case on the needs of his life, then I have sent wheat and barley to him, which he ate himself or distributed to others." And they said "The man is one of us. He drank the waters of our river and he ascended to heaven from our land. Is it right that you who come from somewhere else should take him from our possession? You should know that there is not one of us who will allow it. He will be buried here." The matron replied: "You want to know the origin of his family? He came from another region. You speak of the waters of his river? They did less to quench his thirst than the waters of heaven." And as they exchanged words like this the inhabitants of Lipidiacum dug a grave, placed a sarcophagus there and set about burying the body. But the woman called for help, put the peasants to flight and took away the holy body by force. She placed

---

2. His feast-day is June 24. Lupicinus is one of the few saints in *VP* not to be mentioned in *LH*, so there are no indications of the date. The fact that Gregory stresses that his informant is 80 years old (see last sentence of *VP* XIII) suggests that Lupicinus died in the first half of the sixth century.

3. *Vicus Transaliensis*, cant. Jalligny, arr. Gannat, dép. Allier. A pilgrim from Trézelle is cured at Tours: see *VSM* II 10.

crowds of singers with crosses, candles and incense along the way, and then she had the body placed on a bier and carried to the village of Trézelle.[4] The people saw that and repented, sending a message to the woman which said "We have sinned in resisting you, and we recognise sincerely the will of the Lord in this matter. We ask you now not to exclude us from his funeral service, but to allow us to attend." She allowed them to follow the coffin, and thus the inhabitants of both places united together and went together to Trézelle. Mass was celebrated and the holy body was buried with great honour and joy. The saint has manifested himself there several times by miracles, and his holy work has also been shown many times at Lipidiacum, as we have said, for both these places are protected by the same saint. And perhaps some doubters will try to object to what we have said. But they should know that I have seen the priest Deodatus, who is eighty years old, and he has told me the things which I have written here, declaring under oath that everything is the absolute truth.

---

4. For the history of the idea that success in the theft of relics demonstrates that God approves of the action, see P. Geary, *Furta Sacra* (Princeton, 1978). The body of St Martin of Tours was similarly stolen, from Poitevins by the men of Tours, as Gregory tells in *LH* I 48.

XIV.   About St Martius, an abbot

Divine goodness grants us a great benefit when it orders a refuge to be made for us for the remission of our sins, if we forgive the trespasses of others, if we are indulgent towards those who offend us, if we answer hatred with a blessing, the Lord Jesus Christ having said to us "Love your enemies, do good to them that hate you, and pray for them which despitefully use you and persecute you, that ye may be the children of your Father which is in heaven" (Matthew 5:44-5). Behold the great treasure that you lay up if you despise anger, reconcile yourself to him who has condemned you, absolve him who has judged you. This treasure makes you the son of God the Father, coheir with Christ, and has established you as an inhabitant of the celestial kingdoms. It is thus clear that sins are forgotten in heaven for those who in this world forgive those who have offended them. For this is what Our Lord has said on this matter: "For if ye forgive men their trespasses, your heavenly Father will also forgive you" (Matthew 6:14). And when He teaches His humble servants to pray, He says "You will pray thus to your Father: Forgive us our trespasses as we forgive them that trespass against us" (Matthew 6:9,12).

This blessed abbot, St Martius, was a person celebrated for his holiness, instructed in divine learning, who retained in his heart the good teaching that one should pardon freely the one who has offended you. Not only did he pardon the fault, but he also accompanied the pardon with some present, so as never to cheapen the person of the offender. But we shall first say some words of his life, before speaking of the favour of this grace.

1. The blessed Martius, abbot in the diocese of Clermont, was, it is said, a native of that region. From his childhood he led a religious life, and he consecrated himself entirely to the works of God. He was sober in his eating, generous in his alms, assiduous in his vigils, and very devout in his prayers. He strove with all his might to defeat lust by the bridle of abstinence and the battle of frugality, so that it had not the least hold on him. It was not without reason that he was called Mars, for with the sword of the Holy Spirit as a martial conqueror he slew the swarming thoughts of mortal hostility almost before they had appeared. He was not deaf to the exhortation of the epistle which tells us "Put on

the whole armour of God and the sword of the Holy Spirit, wherewith
ye shall be able to quench the fiery darts of the Enemy" (Ephes.
6:11,17). When he had reached legal majority, and sparkled in his town
like a great star, he nevertheless thought that there was something
lacking. He went some distance away and took a pick and began to
attack a rocky mountain, digging out cells to make himself a small
dwelling-place. He did that so that he might be restrained more strictly
by the chain of sobriety and thus offer more easily to the Almighty God
the incense of his prayers and the sacrifices of his praises on the altar
of a pure heart, recalling the words of the Lord in His Gospel: "Enter
thy closet and when thou hast shut thy door, pray to thy Father, and thy
Father which seeth in secret shall reward thee openly" (Matthew 6:6).
He knew indeed that he would be consoled by the visits of angels if he
removed himself far from the eyes of men. Thus he prepared in that
cave which he had dug into the mountain the things necessary for a
dwelling, forming in the heart of the cave, from the stone itself, a bench
and a bed on which to rest his body when tired from hard work. But all
these things were immovable, since they were cut out of the rock, and
when he wished to rest he put nothing over them except the habit which
he wore, having that as rugs, feathers and blanket. He had nothing of
his own except the worship of God, in which he occupied himself all
the time. The generosity of devout people now and then gave him food.

2.   Finally the eternal Lord, who continually glorifies His
saints, started to make known to men the heavenly merit of His servant
and to show them what sort of man this was who worshipped Him, and
He deigned to grant him the grace of curing the sick. For he chased
demons from the bodies of the possessed, in the name of Jesus Christ,
and he stopped the venom of malignant sores with the sign of the cross.
He also cured those with quartan and tertian fevers with an infusion of
holy oil, and he granted people many other benefits by the will of the
Lord, the dispenser of all good things. Attracted by the fame of such a
great man some men began to gather near him, wishing to instruct
themselves by his teaching. What more need I say? He brought men
together, made them monks, and rendered them perfect in the work of
God. He had very great patience and armed himself with so much
kindness in order to repel the arrows launched to harm him that you
would have thought him protected by a breastplate of gentleness. The

monks had a garden filled with a great quantity of various vegetables and fruit-trees; it was at the same time beautiful to look at and pleasing in its fertility. In the shade of its trees, whose leaves murmured gently at the breath of the wind, the blessed man usually sat. An impatient man, without fear of God and tormented by the desires of gluttony, once forced his way through the hedge of this garden and entered furtively, which the Lord condemns in His Gospel, saying "He that entereth not by the door is a thief and a robber" (John 10:1). It happened during the night, nor could it have been done except at night, for "everyone that doeth evil hateth the light" (John 3:20). This man gathered some vegetables, onions, garlics and fruit, and returned heavy with the burden of his blameworthy deceit to the opening by which he had entered. But he could not find it, and weighed down by the burden he carried and by his own conscience, he uttered deep sighs because of this double burden, and leant now and then on the trunk of one of the trees. He went round and round the whole perimeter of the garden, but not only could he not find the proper entrance but he could not even find the one that he himself had opened in the nocturnal shadows. He was tortured by a double fear, that he might fall into the hands of the monks or that he might be taken by the judge. In the midst of these thoughts the dark of the night departed and the torch of the day, which he did not desire, approached. At that time the abbot used the night for the singing of psalms, and he learnt what had happened by a revelation from God, I believe. As the sky lightened he called the prior of the monastery and said to him "Go quickly to the garden. A frisky ox has entered, but he has not caused any damage. Go up to him and give him what he needs, and then let him go, for it is written in the Scriptures; Thou shalt not muzzle the mouth of the ox that treadeth out the corn (I Corinth. 9:9)." The prior did not understand what the abbot meant, but he went to carry out his orders. The man saw him coming, and threw what he had stolen down to the ground and tried to flee. But he plunged his head into the midst of the thorns and spines, just like a pig, trying to open for himself an entrance by hasty thrusts. The monk seized him and said "Do not fear, my son, for our lord has sent me to lead you out of this place." Then he gathered up all that the man had thrown down, all the fruits and vegetables, and put them on the man's shoulders. Then he opened the gate and took his leave of him, saying "Go in peace, and do not do again such a shameful deed as this."

3. This abbot, illuminating the world like a torch of the pure light, frequently chased away illnesses by the efficacy of his power.

A certain Nivardus suffered for a long time from a fever, and he constantly drank water to appease the fire of his illness, so that he became dropsical, his belly and stomach visibly swelling up, like a bladder. He despaired of his illness, and asked to be brought in a cart to the saint. So he was taken out of bed, put on a cart and pulled to the cell of St Martius, whom he humbly begged to lay his hands on him. The saint, who had been prostrate in prayer in the presence of the Lord, turned towards the sick man and gently touched his body, returning his health to him in the sight of everyone. And it is said that this swelling which afflicted the body of Nivardus disappeared so completely under the fingers of the saint that in the end there remained no trace of the former illness. I heard of these things from my father, for this Nivardus was a great friend of his.

My father told me that he himself had seen the saint. He said that when he was still a child, about eleven years old, he was afflicted with a tertian fever. Friends brought him to the man of God, who was already old and nearing the end of his days, and who could hardly see any more. When he had put his hand on the child he asked, "Who is this, or whose child is it?" He was told "This child is your servant Florentius, son of the late Georgius, the senator." And the holy man said "May the Lord bless you, my son, and may He deign to cure your weakness." The child kissed his hands and thanked him, and went away cured. And he affirmed that for the rest of his life he never again had this illness.

4. At the age of ninety, covered with the sweat of his good fight, he completed the course of his life. Keeping always his faith in God, the saint went elsewhere for that crown of justice which the Lord will give him on the day of judgement.[1] Then his body was washed with great honour and dressed in suitable clothes, and buried in the

---

1. His feast-day is April 13. If he was nearly 90 when he cured the 11-year-old boy who later became Gregory's father, he must have died in the first decade of the sixth century. But we can perhaps be as suspicious about his age as in the case of Patroclus, *VP* IX n.3 above.

oratory of the monastery.[2] That his holy tomb was made famous by the divine miracles that were manifested there can be attested by the crowd of sick people who visit it. They go to the tomb sick and immediately return home cured. And indeed when the sick come there from all sides with various diseases they find a remedy there, and often feel the shivers of fever which agitated their body replaced by a perfect health, by the grace of Our Lord Jesus Christ, who glorifies by illustrious miracles the tombs of the saints, after having formerly recalled some of them from their tombs. To Him be glory for ever and ever! Amen.

---

2. The church of Saint-Mart is mentioned in the tenth century *Libellus de ecclesiis Claromontanis*: it was in what is now the village of Chamalières (Puy-de-Dôme). An inscription was found in the 1870s which appeared to bear Martius' name: regrettably it actually refers to the month of March. See V-T, no. 64.

XV.   About St Senoch, an abbot

"Vanity of vanities, saith the Preacher, all is vanity" (Ecclesiastes 1:2). Is it true that everything which is done in the world is vanity? Because of this it happens that the saints of God, who are burned by no ardour of passions, who are pricked by no goad of concupiscence, who are not polluted by the filth of lust, and who are not even brought down, so to speak, in their thoughts, are nevertheless carried away by the wiles of the Tempter, regarding themselves as perfectly just and in consequence being swollen by the pride of an arrogant presumption. Thus those whom the sword of great crimes has not been able to slay have been easily ruined by the light smoke of vanity. This happened to the man of whom we are going to speak, who, although he shone by many virtues, would certainly have fallen headlong into the abyss of arrogance if he had not been restrained by the careful exhortations of his faithful brothers.

1. The blessed Senoch, a Taifal by birth, was born in the region of Poitou called Theifalia and, having turned towards the Lord, he became a cleric and established a monastery.[1] He found in the territory of Tours old walls, and by restoring them from ruins he made worthy dwellings.[2] He also found an oratory in which, it is said, our illustrious St Martin had prayed. He restored it with much care, and having placed an altar inside which had a small compartment suitable for containing relics, he invited the bishop to come to bless it.[3] The blessed Bishop Eufronius came, and when he had blessed the altar he bestowed on Senoch the honour of the diaconate.[4] They then celebrated

---

1. Senoch is mentioned in *LH* V 7. The Taifals were an Asiatic nomadic people, like the Huns, who were probably settled in Gaul as prisoners-of-war in the third or fourth century. LH IV 18 tells of the revolt of the Taifals of Poitou against Duke Austrapius. The place-name Tiffauges (dép. Deux-Sèvres) derives from Teifalia. See James 1977, pp. 201 and 214. The personal name Senoca has been found inscribed on a sarcophagus from Neuvicq, immediately to the south of Poitou: see L. Maurin, "Le cimetière mérovingien de Neuvicq-Montguyon (Charente-Maritime)", *Gallia* 29 (1971), 151-189.

2. For the archaeological implications, see James 1981 p. 34.

3. Now Saint-Senoch, cant. Ligueil, arr. Tours, dép. Indre-et-Loire. See V-T, no. 269.

4. Eufronius, Gregory's relative and predecessor, was bishop of Tours from 556 to 573.

Mass. But when they wanted to place the casket of relics in the hollow prepared for it they found that the casket was too large and would not go in. Then the deacon fell down and began to pray with the bishop himself, weeping, and he obtained what he asked for. What a marvellous thing! The place which had been too small was enlarged by divine power, and the casket itself grew smaller, so that it entered very easily, to the great amazement of those who were present. Senoch assembled three monks in this place, and served the Lord assiduously. To begin with he walked in the narrow path of life, taking very little food and drinking very little. At the time of holy Lent his abstinence was increased by a diminution of food, for he ate only some barley bread and drank only water, taking just one pound of each of these substances each day. And he was happy in the severity of winter to put no covering on his feet, and he used to attach iron chains to his neck, feet and hands. Then he withdrew from the sight of his brothers to lead a solitary life. He enclosed himself in a cell, praying constantly, passing the days and nights in prayers and vigils, without any pause. The faithful, in their devotion, often brought him money, but instead of hiding it in the ground he put it into the purses of the poor, for he often recalled the words of the Lord, "Lay not up for yourselves treasures upon the earth", for "where your treasure is there will your heart be also" (Matthew 6:19,21). He gave away what he received, for God's sake, in order to relieve the various necessities of the poor. And as a result during his life he delivered from the bonds of servitude and from the burden of debts more than two hundred wretched people.

2. When we arrived in the diocese of Tours he left his cell and came to see us;[5] having greeted us and kissed us he returned home. He had, as we have said, great abstinence, and he cured the sick. But just as his sanctity came from his abstinence, so vanity began to emerge slowly from his sanctity. For he left his cell and went with arrogant pride to visit his family in that area of Poitou which we have mentioned. And on his return he was swollen with pride and sought only to please himself. But when he had been criticised by us and when he had recognised that the proud are far from the kingdom of God, he

---

5. Gregory became bishop in 573, but may not have come to his see immediately.

purged himself entirely of his vanity and made himself so humble that
there remained in him not the smallest trace of pride. And he confessed,
saying "I now recognise the truth of the words spoken by the sacred
mouth of the Apostle, 'He that glorieth let him glory in the Lord' (I
Corinth. 1:31)." But as the Lord worked many miracles of healing
through him, and as he said that he wished to enclose himself so that he
would no longer see the human face, we advised him not to constrain
himself by such seclusion, except only during the days which come
between the death of St Martin and the celebration of Christmas,[6] or
during those other forty days preceding the feast of Easter, which the
authority of the Fathers ordains us to spend in great abstinence. During
the rest of the year he ought to put himself at the disposal of the sick.
He listened to our advice, received our words willingly, and obeyed
them without hesitation.

3. Finally, having said something of the life of this saint, let
us now come to the miracles which it pleased the curing hand of the
Almighty to accomplish through him. A blind man called Popusitus
came to find him (at this time he had already been ordained as priest)
and asked him for something to eat. But his eyes were touched by the
hand of the holy priest with the sign of the cross, and he deserved to
receive the healing sign, for he immediately recovered his sight.

Another boy from Poitou, with the same trouble, heard people
talk about what his confessor had done, and begged him to restore the
light he had lost. Without delay he invoked the name of Christ, and
made the sign of the cross over the eyes of the blind boy. Immediately
blood flowed out in a stream, and light entered, and after twenty years
the torch of day lit the two extinguished stars on the face of this
wretched person. Two boys crippled in all their limbs and twisted up
like round balls were brought into the presence of the saint. When he
had touched them with his hands their limbs straightened, and in the
space of an hour he delivered both of them. Thus he doubled his good
work by a double miracle. A boy and girl were also presented, who had
their hands all contracted. It was in the midst of the Easter celebrations.
They begged the servant of God to remove their affliction, but he

---

6. From November 11 to December 25.

delayed doing what they asked, because of the great crowd of people who had come to the church, and he said aloud that he was not worthy that God should bestow such benefits on the sick through him. But in the end he ceded to the prayers of all, took the hands of these two in his own, and when he had touched them their fingers straightened, and he sent both of them away cured. Likewise a woman called Benaia, who came with her eyes closed and went away with her eyes open, after he had touched them with his healing hand. I do not think I ought to be silent about how often, by his words, he obtained that the venom of serpents should do no evil. Indeed, two people swollen up after having been bitten by a snake came and fell at his feet, praying that he should chase away by his power the venom that the tooth of this wicked beast had spread through their bodies, threatening them with death. The saint prayed to the Lord, saying "Lord Jesus Christ, who, at the beginning, created everything in this world, and who has ordained that the serpent, envious of men, should live under a curse, expel the evil of his venom out of your servants, so that they may triumph over the serpent and not he over them!" Having said these words he stroked all parts of their bodies, and soon the swelling went down and the murderous venom lost its strength to harm.

The day of Our Lord's resurrection had come. A man was going to church and saw a herd of animals ruining his crops. He groaned, and says "Woe on me, for the work of my whole year is being wasted and nothing will remain." And he took an axe and began to cut branches to block the opening in the hedge. Immediately, of its own accord, his hand gripped itself so that it could not release what it had grasped. In great pain, the man ran to find the holy confessor, dragging behind him the branch that his hand had seized, and told him just what had happened. Then he rubbed holy oil on the man's hand, and pulled out the branch, and cured him. After that he cured many people of the bite of serpents and the poison of malignant pustules, by making the sign of the cross over them. Others, tormented by the hatred of the savage demon, recovered their full senses as soon as he had laid his hands on them, chasing the demons away. And to all those whom the hand of God cured from various diseases through him he cheerfully gave in addition food and clothing if they were in need. He took so much care of those in need that he diligently built bridges across rivers, so that no-one would fear cruel drowning during the seasons of floods.

4. This holy man was thus made illustrious in the world by such miracles. Having attained the age of about forty years he was taken by a small fever which kept him in bed for about three days. Someone then announced to me that his end was near. I hurried to his bedside, but I was not able to get any word out of him, for he was very weak, and after about an hour he gave up the spirit.[7] To his funeral came that crowd of people whom he had ransomed, that is to say, those whom we have mentioned whom he freed from either servitude or debt, and those whom he had nourished or clothed. They mourned, saying "To whom do you leave us, holy father?"[8] Later, when he was lying in his grave, he often manifested himself by evident miracles. The thirtieth day after his death, when Mass was being celebrated at his tomb, a paralysed man called Chaidulf, who had come to ask for alms, recovered the use of his limbs as soon as he had kissed the cloth which covered the tomb. I have known many other miracles which happened in this place, but I think that these things are enough to recall his memory.[9]

---

7. In 576, as is clear from *LH* V 7. His feast-day is on October 24.

8. Cf. Sulpicius Severus, *Epist.* 3 on the death of Martin, *GC* 104 on the death of St Radegund, and *VP* XIX 4.

9. Gregory adds another miracle-tale in his chapter on Senoch in *GC* 25.

XVI.   About St Venantius, an abbot

Heavenly power bestows on the churches and on the peoples of the earth a present both unique and multiple, when it continually grants to the world not only those who can intercede for sinners but also those who can teach about eternal life. Thus what appears to be only a single gift is nevertheless multiple when it is given by the divine majesty, because all those who have wished to ask have received in abundance, following these words: "Ask and ye shall receive" (John 16:24), et cetera. Thus the human mind must carefully and constantly investigate the life of the saints, so that, incited by that study and inflamed by that example, it might always turn to what it knows to be pleasing to God and so that it might either merit to be delivered by Him or be able to be heard. The saints have sought to receive these things from the divine majesty, continually begging Him that He should enter their heart, that He should make them perfect in their work, that He should speak in their mouths, that their minds might be purged more easily in though, word and deed and might think in holiness, speak in justice and act with honesty. From which it results that when they submitted themselves to what would be pleasing to God, they obtained the remission of the debt of sin, they were snatched from the contagious filth of vice and were invited, because of their merit, to enter the heavenly kingdom. They set before their eyes the examples of their predecessors, and they praised the Almighty Lord together, because of the love of those, as we have said, whom they choose to take as their models. And we too, in trying to say something in celebration of the devout servant of God, the abbot St Venantius, rather return to God His own gifts, for it is clear that His right hand has accomplished what He wishes the saints to have done. We beg Him to open the mouth of a dumb man so that the deeds of this cleric may be made known, for if we are indeed very deficient in knowledge, we do at least know in our own conscience that we are a sinner.

1.   St Venantius lived in the city of Bourges, and his parents were, according to secular rank, of free birth, and catholics. Having arrived at the age of youth his parents engaged him in the bonds of betrothal. As happens with those of his age, he began to love the young

girl. He used to bring her presents of cups, and also shoes.[1] Then it came to him, by the inspiration of God, to go to Tours. There was then a monastery near the basilica of St Martin, where Abbot Silvinus governed, by the sceptre of a rule, a flock consecrated to the service of God.[2] The holy man went there and, seeing the virtues of St Martin, said to himself "It seems to me that it would be better to serve Christ without blemish than to be involved through the bonds of matrimony with the pollution of the world. I shall abandon my betrothed from the land of Bourges and I shall join through faith the Catholic Church, so that I shall not deceive by my deeds the feelings which I have in my heart." Meditating along those lines, he came to the abbot and threw himself at his feet, and told him his innermost feelings, weeping as he did so. And the abbot thanked God for the faith of this boy and addressing him a priestly speech he tonsured the youth and admitted him into the monastic flock. From that moment he showed himself full of humility towards his brothers, and full of charity towards everyone, and he arrived at such a high degree of saintliness that all were as fond of him as if he were their own kinsman. Thus, when the abbot died, he was called by the choice of the brothers to replace him.

2. One Sunday, invited to celebrate the sacrifice of the Mass, he said to the brothers, "Already my eyes are covered by shadows, and I can no longer read the book. Ask another priest to do these things." While the priest officiated, the holy man stood very near him, and when the moment arrived at which, according to catholic custom, the holy offering had to be blessed by the sign of the cross, he saw as if at one window of the apse a ladder, down which seemed to descend a venerable old man, honoured with the marks of the clericature, who with his outstretched hand blessed the sacrifice offered on the altar. These things happened in the basilica of St Martin; but nobody merited the sight of them except him, and we do not know why the others did not see anything. Afterwards he told this to the brothers, and there is no doubt that the Lord had allowed his faithful servant to see these things,

---

1. Gifts of shoes after betrothal is mentioned also in *VP* XX 1.

2. Called *abbatiola S. Venantii* in tenth-century charters. Remains of the monastery were possibly discovered in the former place St-Venant in Tours in 1941: see V-T no. 320.

and had deigned to reveal to him the secrets of celestial mysteries. The same Venantius, indeed, was returning one Sunday from the basilica of the saints, after completing his prayers, supported on his stick, and he stopped still in the middle of the forecourt of the church of the holy confessor, listening carefully, his eyes turned for a long time towards heaven. Then, stepping forward a few paces, he began to groan and to sigh. Asked by those who accompanied him what it was, and to tell them if he had seen some divine thing, he replied "Woe on us apathetic and idle creatures! I see that in heaven the solemnity of Mass is far advanced, while we are so dilatory that we have not even heard the voices of the angels in heaven, singing 'Sanctus!' and proclaiming the praises of the Lord." Then he ordered Mass to be said immediately in the monastery. I would also like to mention another occasion, when he was returning from the churches after having said prayers there, as was his custom (as I have said before). Mass was being celebrated in the basilica, and when the words from the Lord's Prayer "Deliver us from evil" were sung, he heard a voice from a tomb which said also "Deliver us from evil." One must believe that he who deserved to hear that was a man of special merit. It was also given to him, when he visited the tomb of the priest Passivus, to learn from him the nature of his merits and the amount of his heavenly joy.

3. Although these are great things, I wish to turn now to talk of the grace which, through him, the Lord granted to the sick. There is no doubt that through him, as we have said above, the right hand of God acted, when He made to him such great revelations as we have reported. A young boy called Paul, who suffered great pains in the shins and knees, came to find the saint, and throwing himself at his feet he began to beg him to obtain a cure for him from the mercy of God, by his prayer. The saint immediately prayed; then he rubbed the limbs of the sick boy with holy oil and made him rest on his bed. At the end of an hour he ordered him to get up. The child got up, and by the hands of the saint was returned cured to his mother. The slave of a certain Faretrus, who hated his master, fled into the oratory of this priest. The master, filled with pride and profiting from the absence of the holy man, took his servant and slew him. But soon after he was seized by a fever and breathed his last. Very often by his prayers the saint cured quartan, tertian and other fevers. By the saving sign of the cross he combatted

the poison in malignant pustules, and by invoking the name of the Trinity he cleansed those possessed by demons. Often he had to struggle against demons, but he always emerged the victor. Rising from his bed one night to go to say the office, he saw two great rams standing in front of his door, as if they had expected his coming, and as soon as they saw him they threw themselves at him with fury. But he opposed them with the sign of the cross, and saw them disappear, and he entered his oratory without fear. Another night, returning from the oratory, he found his cell full of demons, and he said to them "Where do you come from?" "From Rome," they replied. "We left yesterday in order to come here." And he said to them "Withdraw, detestable creatures, and do not approach a place in which the name of God is invoked!" At these words the demons vanished like smoke.

4. The man who had received the grace of accomplishing great miracles and other similar things, after having completed the course of this present life, left the world in order to receive eternal life, and his tomb is often glorified by illustrious miracles.[3]

A wicked demon had troubled the spirit of Mascarpion, a servant of the monastery, who was possessed for three years and used to come to rave in front of the tomb of the holy man. In the end he was, we believe, delivered of this demon by the prayer of the blessed man, and he lived for long years quite sane in his mind. The wife of Julian, who was oppressed by a quartan fever, was delivered from all fire and from all shivering as soon as she touched the tomb of the holy man, and she left cured. The wife of Baudimund was in the same state, and she was cured as soon as she had fallen down and prayed beside the bed of the same saint.[4] We have heard many other things about him, but those which we have written are sufficient, we think, to establish belief in the minds of catholics.

---

3. His feast-day is October 13. He died in the fifth century, for some time later Licinius became abbot of this monastery before becoming bishop of Tours in 507: *LH* X 31(8).

4. There are similar miracles mentioned by Gregory at *GC* 15, which is a much shorter account of Venantius.

XVII.   About St Nicetius, bishop of the Treveri

If we believe what is spoken, then I think we should faithfully believe those who tell us of holy works done for the sake of the faith, for we have not ourselves seen everything which we have read in books. Some things are believed because they have been confirmed by someone's written account, some are proven by the testimony of other writers, and some indeed we believe by the authority of our own eyes. But there are people who by a perversion of the intelligence do not believe what is written, find fault with what is witnessed by others, and even scorn as fraudulent what they themselves have seen. They do not even have that trust which the apostle St Thomas had in his heart when he said "Except I shall see, I will not believe." "Blessed are they that have not seen, and yet have believed" (John 20:25,29). As soon as Thomas had seen, straightway he believed. But, as we have said, there are many who not only do not believe the things that they have seen, but attempt to tear out the very foundations of belief from their own breasts. Thus, in proposing to write something on the virtues, courage, grandeur of soul and sanctity of St Nicetius, bishop of Trier, I fear that I shall be criticised by some, who will say "You are a young man, so how can you know about the deeds of those in the past? How has what they have done come to your knowledge? Surely the things that you have written can only be regarded as fictions made up by you." This is why it is necessary to make known the narrator of what I have learnt, so as to confound those who disparage the truth. May they know that I have heard the things reported below from the holy Aredius, abbot of Limoges, who was raised by St Nicetius himself and who received clerical orders from him.[1] And I do not believe that he could be deceived, for at the time he was telling me these things God was through him bringing light to the eyes of the blind, allowing the paralytic to walk and giving reason to the possessed, after having chased

---

1. The "Life" of St Aredius is inserted by Gregory at *LH* X 29, on the occasion of his death in 591. He was from Limoges, entered Theudebert's entourage, and was persuaded by Nicetius to join the clergy. He returned to Limoges on his father's death, built churches and founded a monastery, at the place now called St Yrieux. There is a Carolingian *Life of Aredius* (ed. Krusch *MGH SSRM* III pp. 576-609), once thought to be by Gregory of Tours.

out the demons which assailed them. Nor is it believable that he could be obscured by the cloud of a lie, he whom God often protected so well against the clouds of rain that he was not touched by a single drop of rain which fell, even though those who accompanied him were completely drenched.[2] Finally, if one denies such a witness one also has to distrust the favours of God. The priest I have named said of the bishop in question, "It is true, gentle brother, that I have known many things of St Nicetius by the witness of good people, but I have seen more with my own eyes, or I have learnt them from the saint himself, although I have had to drag them out of him with difficulty. And when he explained clearly those things which God had deigned to accomplish by him, he was not raised up by the buskin of vainglory, but spoke with compunction in his heart and tears in his eyes, saying: My dearest son, I wish to tell you these things so that, living with a great innocence of heart, you may mediate upon such things. For nobody can raise himself to the height of God's miracles unless 'he hath clean hands and a pure heart' (Ps. 24:4), as David sang in his poem." Having thus spoken, he began his tale.

1. The holy Bishop Nicetius was destined from the moment of his birth for the clergy. As soon as he had been born one could see that his head was completely deprived of hair, as is often the case with the newly born, but that there was a ring of down all around his head, so that one would have thought from that ring that he had been granted the clerical tonsure.[3] Because of that, his parents brought him up with great care, instructed him in letters and sent him to the abbot of a monastery. There he showed himself to be so devoted to the Lord that when the abbot died he succeeded him. Having taken over office he conducted himself in such a way as regards instruction and correction that not only

---

2. A miracle mentioned in *LH* X 29. It happened "not long ago", that is, not long before Aredius' last visit to Tours and subsequent death in 591. *VP* XVII must have been written 591 or 592, and presumably after Aredius had died.

3. A very early use of the word *corona* to describe a clerical tonsure. It suggests that in Gregory's day the corona was regarded as the normal form, but we cannot use this story as evidence that in Nicetius' day this was necessarily so. I have argued for a late development of the "orthodox" tonsure: see "Bede and the tonsure question", *Peritia* 3 (1984), 85-98.

did he not permit the brothers to do anything wrong, but not even to
speak wrongly, saying "My beloved, you must avoid jokes and all idle
words; for, just as we have to present to God our body entirely pure, so
we ought not to open our mouths unless it is to praise God. There are
three ways by which a man is ruined: when he thinks, when he speaks
or when he acts. Therefore, my beloved, avoid levity, malice and every
other evil." He exhorted his brothers in this way and in others, so as to
make them pure and worthy of God. He was very respected and
honoured by King Theuderic, because he had often revealed to him his
sins, in order to improve him through his reprimands. And because of
that, when the bishop of Trier died, the king offered Nicetius the
bishopric.[4] And with the consent of the people and by the decree of the
king he was led to his consecration by men honoured with the highest
dignities at the royal court. They arrived near the town at sunset, and as
the sun was starting to go down they put up their tents and prepared
their camp, and they let their horses go free so that they could feed in

---

4. This is an event already mentioned, in *VP* VI 3: the king is Theuderic and the bishop
is Aprunculus. Nicetius became bishop at the same time that Gallus became bishop of
Clermont, in 525: Gregory does not mention in *VP* XVII that the Treveri wanted Gallus
for their bishop rather than Nicetius. Note that Gregory calls Nicetius bishop of "the
Treveri", not "of Trier" (cf. the invariable usage in early medieval royal titles, where kings
are kings of peoples not of territories); the other Nicetius (*VP* VIII) is bishop of a civitas,
Lyons. As Ian Wood has pointed out to me, this contributes to the evidence which
suggests that Trier and other north-east Gallic dioceses, such as Mainz, no longer
conformed to the Roman civitas structure.

 Theuderic and other Austrasian kings seem to have been interested in importing
Aquitanian clerics to the Rhineland, presumably in an attempt to raise the standard of the
clergy there: see E. Ewig, "L'Aquitaine et les pays rhénans au haut moyen âge" in his
Spätantikes und fränkisches Gallien, I (Munich, 1976), pp. 553-72. On p. 560 he notes
that later Trier tradition made Nicetius out to be from the Limousin, which would explain
the connection with Aredius of Limoges. The impact of Aquitanians on the north-east of
the kingdom is also discussed by Rouche, pp. 433-41.

 It is worth noting that Nicetius is one of the earliest Merovingian ecclesiastics
to be shown castigating his monarch for his sins (following the model of St Martin of
Tours, as reported by Sulpicius Severus: see Stancliffe, esp. pp. 156-7). He was to be
followed in this risky exercise by Desiderius of Vienne and the Irishman Columbanus,
who were like Nicetius both sent into exile as a result, the former to meet his
"martyrdom" (on which see J. Fontaine, "King Sisebut's *Vita Desiderii* and the political
function of Visigothic hagiography", in E. James, ed., *Visigothic Spain: new approaches*
(Oxford, 1980), pp. 93-129).

the fields of poor people. When he saw that, the blessed Nicetius was touched with compassion and said "Withdraw those horses from the poor men's crops immediately, or I shall withdraw you from communion." They replied indignantly, "Why do you say that? You are not yet a bishop and already you threaten us with excommunication?" He said, "I tell you in truth that the king has taken me out of my monastery and ordered me to undertake this office. Certainly the will of God will be accomplished, for I shall make sure that the will of the king will never be done if he wishes evil." And he went quickly forward and chased the horses from the field, and he was led to the town in the midst of these men's admiration. He never honoured the persons of the great, but feared God alone, both in his thoughts and in his deeds. One day, while he was sitting on his episcopal throne and listening to the succession of readings, he felt I know not what sort of weight on his neck. He tried to feel it secretly two or three times with his hand, but he could not discover what this weight was. Then, turning his head to left and to right, he smelt a sweet odour, and understood that this weight was the burden of episcopal dignity.

2. As soon as he was bishop he showed himself to be terrible towards those who did not observe the commands of God; in a stentorian voice he proclaimed their imminent death. At this point I think I should say some words to fortify the censure of priests, either for the instruction of the people or else for the reform of the way of life of kings. On the death of Theuderic his son Theudebert took over the kingdom, and did many unjust things, on the subject of which the bishop berated him very often, either if he himself was the malefactor or if he did not reprove those who had committed crimes.[5] One Sunday the king entered church with people whom the pontiff had excommunicated. After he had read the lessons prescribed by ancient canons and the offerings had been placed on the altar of God, the bishop says "We will not carry on with the celebration of Mass today unless those deprived of communion leave the church." The king wanted to resist this; and suddenly a young man in the congregation,

---

5.   Theudebert succeeded his father in 534. On him see Collins 1983: he discusses Nicetius, pp. 22-5. On the other hand in LH III 25 Gregory says that Theudebert was a great king, virtuous, just, respecting his bishops, generous to the churches and to the poor.

seized by a demon, cries out and begins to confess in a loud voice, in
the midst of the pains of his torment, both the virtues of the saint and
the crimes of the king. He said that the bishop was chaste and the king
was an adulterer;[6] that the former was humble in his fear of Christ, and
the latter was proud in his royal glory; that the priest would be
discovered by God without blemish and the other would soon be
destroyed by the author of his crimes. And when the frightened king
asked that the possessed man be sent out of the church, the bishop said
"Firstly those who follow you, that is to say, the incestuous, the
murderers and the adulterers, must be expelled from the church, and
then God will ordain that this man be silent." Immediately the king gave
the order that all those who had been condemned by episcopal sentence
should leave the church. Afterwards the bishop ordered the demoniac to
be expelled also. But he clung to a column, and ten men could not drag
him away from it. Then the saint of God made the sign of the cross
(under his vestments, lest he attract vainglory to himself), and
commanded the demon to free him. Immediately the man fell to the
ground together with those who were pulling him with all their strength,
and after a little while he stood up, cured. After the ceremony he was
sought for, but could not be found, and nobody was ever able to
discover where he had come from or gone to. Many people concluded
that he had been sent by God in order to make the deeds of the king
and of the bishop known. After that, at the prayer of the bishop, the
king showed himself to be more gentle, so that the pastor worthy of
reward by God might hear the prophecy "If thou take forth the precious
from the vile, thou shalt be as my mouth" (Jerem. 15:19). The holy
bishop preached each day to the people, uncovering the vices of each
and praying continually for the remission of those who confessed. Thus
the venom of hatred often arose against him, because he so truly
proclaimed the wicked deeds of many. Several times he presented
himself voluntarily to the persecutors and offered his neck to the raised
sword; but God did not allow him to come to any harm. For he wished
to die for justice, if he had found a cruel enough enemy for that; he

---

6. Presumably because he had married Deuteria and broken his betrothal to Wisigard: this
was very unpopular with the Franks, according to Gregory LH III 27, who also reports
some scandal about Deuteria in LH III 26. Collins 1983 does not discuss Theudebert's
marital ventures.

used to say "I would willingly die for justice!" He also excommunicated King Chlothar several times for his unjust deeds, and he was never afraid of the exile with which he was threatened.

3. One day he was indeed sent into exile, and was rejected by the other bishops, who were all flatterers of the king, and was abandoned by all those close to him. He says to a deacon who alone persisted in remaining loyal to him, "What are you doing? Why do you not follow your brothers, and do what you wish, as the others do?" He replies, "My Lord God lives, and while there is a breath left in my body I shall not abandon you." "Because you say that", the bishop said, "I wish to reveal to you what it has pleased God to make known to me. Tomorrow at this hour I will take up again the honour which was taken from me, and I will be restored to my church. Those who left me shall return to me with great shame." The deacon was astonished, and waited to see if those words would be proved correct. As the following day dawned an envoy from King Sigibert suddenly came, bearing letters and announcing the death of King Chlothar.[7] Sigibert wrote that he was going to take possession of his kingdom, and that he would like to have the friendship of the bishop. Learning this the bishop returned to his church, entered again into his position, to the great confusion of those who had abandoned him, although he received them all kindly. Who could now say how much strength he had in preaching, how much vigour in discussion, how much constancy in the struggle, and wisdom in instruction? He had indeed always an equal strength in misfortune and in prosperity, without fearing menaces nor being deceived by flattery. For truly (as St Aredius, who told me these things, used to say) like St Paul he was not injured although he was exposed to "perils of waters, perils of robbers, perils in the city, perils among false brethren" (II Corinth. 11:26), et cetera. One day he crossed the Moselle in a boat, and he was pushed by the current between the piles of a bridge. Gripping one pile with his hands he held the boat with his foot, so that, although on the point of drowning, he could be snatched up by those who watched. This must have been a trap of the Tempter. And indeed

---

7. Chlothar I died in 561, in the 51st year of his reign — from which fact derives much of the traditional dating for the reign of his father Clovis.

the author of every crime appeared many times before his eyes as if to harm him.

One day while on a journey he descended from his horse to answer a call of nature among thick bushes, and behold! there appeared to him a frightful shade, of great height, of huge size, black in colour, with an immense number of sparkling eyes, like those of a furious bull, and a large mouth that stood open as if ready to eat up the man of God. But when he made the sign of the cross against it, it vanished like ascending smoke. There is no doubt that the prince of crime had shown himself to him.

4. He was, as we have said, extremely firm in his fasting. For while others took their meal, he would often walk around the basilicas of the saints, accompanied by a single servant, with his head hidden in his hood, lest he be recognised in public. God also gave him the grace of healing. As he was walking one day around the dwellings of the saints, as we have just said, he came to the church of St Maximin the Bishop, in the forecourt of which three possessed men rested, overcome by sleep after many convulsions.[8] Seeing them fast asleep he made over them the sign of the cross, and immediately they woke up, uttering great cries, and suddenly vomiting, they were delivered.

When the bubonic plague was cruelly assailing the population within the walls of the city of Trier,[9] the priest of God assiduously implored divine mercy for the sheep entrusted to him. Suddenly, in the night, a great noise was heard, like a violent clap of thunder which broke above the bridge over the river, so that one would have thought that the town was going to split in two. And all the people were lying in their beds, filled with terror and hiding from the coming of death. And one could hear in the midst of the noise a voice clearer than the others, saying "What must we do, companions? For at one of the gates Bishop Eucherius watches, and at the other Maximin is on the alert.

---

8. On the church of St Maximin, see n.10 below.

9. Perhaps the outbreak of 543; see above n.18 to *VP* VI. Gregory does not mention this incident, or any other in Nicetius' life, in *LH*, which suggests that he knew nothing of him until his conversation(s) with Abbot Aredius, by which time he had written most of LH.

Nicetius is busy in the middle.[10] There is nothing left for us to do except leave this town to their protection." As soon as this voice had been heard, the malady ceased, and from that moment no-one else died. Thus we cannot doubt that the town had been protected by the power of the bishop. He was invited one day by the king, and he said to his men "Go and find a great quantity of fish, so that when we go to meet the king we shall have something with which to acquit our duty, and also minister to our friends." And they told him, "Our fish-trap, where the fish normally come, is thought to be completely empty, and its frames are swept from their places by the force of the river. So it is impossible to carry out your orders, since there is nothing to be found." The saint listened to this, and then went into his cell and called a servant, saying "Go and tell the head-cook to take fish from the river." He did what he was told, and the cook made fun of him. The messenger returned, and the bishop said "I see that you took the message that I gave you, and that no-one wanted to listen to you. Go again and tell them to go." And after they had unwillingly received the same order two or three times, they eventually went, angrily, to the fish-trap, and looking in it they found it so full of fish that ten men would hardly have been able to carry away what was there. Divine power often showed Nicetius things which were useful to him.

5. I must say something of what the Lord revealed to him about the kings of the Franks. He saw one night in a dream a great tower, so high that it almost reached heaven. It had a great number of windows through which angels watched, while God Himself stood at its summit. One of the angels held in his hand a great book, and he said

---

10. The church of St Eucherius (now St Matthias) is outside the north gate of Trier (the famous Porta Nigra) (see V-T, no. 329), and St Maximin is outside the south gate (see V-T, no. 330). The cathedral is between the two, within the walls. Eucherius was the first bishop of Trier, in the third century. Gregory mentions Maximin, bishop of Trier, very briefly in *LH* I 37, as a saint of great influence at the time of the Emperor Constans (mid-fourth century). At *GC* 91 Gregory describes a priest who swears a false oath at the tomb of St Maximin, and then is struck down by a fever before he reached the third door of the crypt. Excavations have shown these two extra-mural churches to be surrounded by large late Roman and Merovingian cemeteries. For up-to-date plans of Trier and a discussion of the St-Maximin excavations, see now H. Cüppers, ed. *Die Römer in Rheinland-Pfalz* (Stuttgart, 1990), pp. 577ff, esp. pp. 641-646.

"This king will live so many years, and this king will live so many years", and he named one king after another, not only those who were then living but also those yet to be born, and he announced the nature of their reign, and the length of their life. When he called the name of each one the other angels replied "Amen." And for each king it happened just as Nicetius declared in his revelation.

Nicetius was once returning from the king by ship, and he slept. And the river was roused by the wind and began to rise in high waves, so that it looked as if the boat was going to sink. And the bishop still slept, as we have said, making that noise that many sleepers do, as if he were oppressed by something.[11] He was woken by those who surrounded him, made the sign of the cross on the water, and the tempest ceased. Then, since he was sighing repeatedly, his men asked him what he had seen. He told them, "I had resolved to be silent, but I will speak. It seemed to me that I cast nets over the whole world, to fish, and my only helper was this young Aredius." And it is fitting that the Lord wished to show him as a caster of nets, for every day he caught congregations at the divine office.

There came to him a man who had very long hair and a long beard, who threw himself at his feet and said "I am he, master, who found himself in danger on the sea, and was delivered by your help." And the saint told him to say why he wished to give him the glory for that: "Tell me how God saved you from this danger, for my power could not have aided anyone." The man replied, "Recently I embarked on a ship in order to go to Italy, and a great number of pagans came with me, and I was the only Christian amid that multitude of pagans.[12] A tempest arose, and I began to invoke the name of the Lord, and to beg Him that your intercession might save me from death. The pagans, for their part, called on their gods, one cried to Jupiter, another to Mercury, another besought the help of Minerva, another one of Venus.

---

11. Reading *sonus* (sound) with MS 4, and not *somnus* (dream), as Krusch, at Dr Gibson's suggestion, and thus seeing it as an elaborate way of saying that he was snoring.

12. Not necessarily proof that Gallo-Roman paganism was still widespread in Gaul, as some have argued. The Roman names for gods do not exclude these travellers being Germans of some kind (cf. the pagan Frankish king Clovis, worshipping Jupiter, Mars and Mercury, according to Gregory, *LH* II 29: surely because of Latin literary conventions rather than any Romanising tendency on Clovis' part).

And as we were in mortal danger, I say to them 'Men! Stop calling on them, for they are not gods but demons. If you want to be saved from this danger, call on St Nicetius, so that he may obtain that you will be saved by the mercy of God.' With one voice they shouted 'God of Nicetius, save us!' And then the sea was calmed, the wind fell, the sun reappeared and our ship carried on its voyage. And I made a vow that I should not cut the hair of my head until I had presented myself in your sight." Then this man went to Clermont, where he said he came from, having cut his hair on the bishop's orders.[13]

There are innumerable things which Abbot Aredius told me about this man, but I think that I must finish this book.

6.   When he knew that the moment for his departure approached, he talked to his brothers, saying "I have seen the apostle Paul with John the Baptist, inviting me to eternal rest and showing me a crown adorned with celestial pearls, and they said to me: Here are the things that you are going to enjoy in the kingdom of God." He reported these words to certain faithful people and then, a few days later, after having contracted a light fever, he surrendered his soul to God, and was buried in the church of St Maximin the bishop.[14] His tomb is today famous for the divine miracles that are done there.[15]

---

13. This should perhaps be translated as "tonsured": entering the clergy as a thanksgiving for some miraculous happening is not unknown in the hagiographical record — cf. Gregory himself in *VP* II 2.

14. His death is not mentioned in *LH*. His feast-day is December 5. He died after 561, as he returned from exile on Chlothar's death in that year (above, *VP* XVII 3), and he wrote to Queen Chlodesinda, grand-daughter of Clovis and wife of the Lombard king, c.564: this letter is translated in Hillgarth pp. 78-9. Venantius Fortunatus wrote a poem about Nicetius (*Carm.* III 11), praising him for his generosity towards the poor and prisoners, for his role as peace-maker, and for restoring churches. He also wrote about the castle Nicetius built overlooking the Moselle (III 12), with its thirty towers, its water led by conduits, which turn a water-mill, and the vines which Nicetius planted on formerly barren hill-sides (an interest which has, for some historians, proved his Aquitanian origins!).

15. For the miracles see *GC* 92.

XVIII. About Ursus and Leobatius, abbots

When the Legislator and Prophet began to speak of the beginning of all things and to show the Lord forming with the majesty of his
right hand the extent of the heavens, he added "and God made two great
lights and the stars, and He set them in the firmament of the heavens to
give light upon the earth" (Genesis 1:16-7). Likewise in the firmament
of human understanding He has placed, as the authority of the Holy
Fathers affirms, two great lights, that is to say Christ and His Church,
so that they may cast light on the darkness of ignorance and illumine
our humble intelligence, as John the Evangelist says of the Lord
Himself: "That was the true light, which lighteth every man that cometh
into the world" (John 1:9). He also put into it the stars, that is to say the
patriarchs, prophets and apostles, who instruct us by their teaching or
enlighten us by their miracles, as He says Himself in the Gospel, "Ye
are the light of the world" (Matthew 5:14), and again "Let your light so
shine before men that they may see your good works and glorify your
Father which is in heaven" (Matthew 5:16). For these apostles are
accepted by their merit on behalf of the whole church, which lives
unpolluted, without spot or blemish, as the Apostle says, "That he might
present it to himself a pure church, not having spot or wrinkle, or any
such thing" (Ephes. 5:27). Then thanks to this doctrine there have been
up until our times men who were like the torches of stars in this world,
not only resplendent by the light of their virtues but also shining by the
greatness of their teaching, who have lit the whole universe with the
rays of their preaching, going to teach in every place, founding
monasteries for the worship of God and instructing men to abstain from
earthly cares and, having left the darkness of concupiscence, to follow
the true God, the creator of all things. This is shown by the stories told
by trustworthy brothers concerning the abbots Ursus and Leobatius.

1. Abbot Ursus was an inhabitant of the city of Cahors, and
from the start of his life he was very devout and filled with the love of
God. He left Cahors and came to the land of Berry, where he founded

monasteries at Tausiriacus, Onia and Pontiniacus.[1] When he had placed them under the rule of priors recommended by their sanctity of life and their wisdom, he went into the Touraine and came to a place which someone had formerly called Senaparia.[2] He built an oratory, founded a monastery, and left the prior Leobatius there, charging him to enforce the rule. Then he went on to found yet another monastery, that is now called Loches, on the river Indre, in the hollow of a hill above which now stands a fortification which bears the same name as the monastery.[3] There, having established a congregation of monks, he resolved not to go to another place, but to work there with his own hands together with the whole community, and to win his daily bread by the sweat of his brow, commending to his brothers among other things what Paul the Apostle says: "Labour with your hands, that ye may have to give to him that needeth" (Ephes. 4:28). And elsewhere, "If any would not work, neither should he eat" (II Thess. 3:10). The Lord granted him the grace of healing, so that with the breath of his mouth alone he chased demons from the bodies of the possessed; He deigned also to accomplish other miracles through him. Ursus was devoted to abstinence in food and drink, and ceaselessly urged his monks to turn their eyes and thoughts from any excess.

2. While he was doing these things, his brothers were grinding the grain necessary for their food by turning the quernstone by hand. He had the idea of lessening their fatigue by building a mill in the bed of the river Indre. He had piles driven into the river, and collected a mass of great stones and made a dam and a channel for the water, whose force would turn the mill-wheel with great speed. Thus he lessened the

---

1. *Tausiriacus* is possibly *Tausiliacus*, Toiselay, next to Châtillon-sur-Indre, arr. Châteauroux, dép. Indre (see V-T, no. 299); *Onia* probably gives us "Heugnes", the name of a forest in the canton of Ecueille, arr. Châteauroux, dép. Indre (V-T, no. 116); *Pontiniacus* is unidentifiable.

2. Now Sennevières, 8 km from Loches, where there is a Romanesque church dedicated to St Leobatius (Leubais).

3. *Loccis*, now Loches, dép. Indre-et-Loire. A church was built here by Bishop Eustochius of Tours (443-60) (*LH* X 31(5)). See C. Lelong, "Recherches sur l'ancienne église Saint-Ours de Loches", *Bulletin Monumentale* 1974, pp. 189-99, for a report of his excavations under the present Romanesque church. See V-T, no. 128.

work of the monks, so that only one brother was needed for this task. But a Goth called Silarius, one of King Alaric's favourites,[4] was envious of the monastery and said to the abbot, "Give me this mill, so that it can be under my control, and I will give you what you want in return." The abbot replied, "Our poverty established this mill after great trouble; we cannot give it away now, lest my brothers die of hunger." "If you wish to give it to me willingly", said Silarius, "I shall thank you for it. Otherwise I shall take it by force, or I shall make another one for which I shall have to divert the water by dams, and your wheel will no longer turn." The abbot replied, "You will not do what God does not wish, and you will certainly not take this mill from us." Then Silarius, boiling with anger, made another machine like the other, upstream of it. And the water built up behind the monastic mill-wheel and made a whirlpool, so that it was unable to turn as before, and the mill was useless. The warden of the mill came to find the abbot, at about midnight, it is said, and found him keeping vigils with his brothers in the oratory. He said, "Come, father, and pray devoutly to the Lord, for the wheel of our mill has stopped because of the flood coming from the new channel that Silarius has made." And the abbot sent a brother to each of the monasteries he had founded, to tell the monks, "Throw yourself down in prayer, and do nothing else until I send news to you." He himself did not leave the oratory, and he prayed devoutly to the

---

4. Alaric II was the Visigothic king who ruled in south-west Gaul and Spain from 484 until his defeat by Clovis and death in 507; see *PLRE* 2 p. 49. Silarius appears in the MSS of *VP* also as Sichlarius and (invariably in MS 4) Salarius. Ursus' monastic confederation seems to have been founded within the Arian Visigothic kingdom. This idea of a monastic federation, with one abbot and priors in each of the daughter houses, does not seem to be at all common in early monasticism, which makes this a particularly important Life. For a rash suggestion concerning possible links with Irish practice, see E. James, "Ireland and western Gaul in the Merovingian period", in D. Whitelock, R. McKitterick and D.N. Dumville, eds., *Ireland in Early Mediaeval Europe* (Cambridge, 1982), p. 269.
    This text is one of the few which shows us that Visigoths were exercising a real presence as far north as the Loire. Gregory shows, in *LH* II 35, Alaric II meeting Clovis on an island in the Loire in the civitas of Tours, which the two kings were perhaps regarding as neutral territory on the border of their two kingdoms. It is also, of course, one of the few early medieval texts giving us any information about the use and importance of water-mills, and has often been discussed in this context, e.g. in M. Bloch, "The advent and triumph of the water-mill" in id., *Land and Work in Medieval Europe* (London, 1967), pp. 136-68.

Lord, waiting for His mercy to come. This went on for two whole days and nights. The third day was beginning to break when the monk who looked after the mill came to say that the wheel was turning as before with great speed. Then the abbot left the oratory with his brothers, approached the river, and looked for the mill that Silarius had built, but could not see it. He came closer to the bank and looked down into the river-bed, but saw no trace of the mill, and nobody ever saw either wood, or stone, or iron, or anything from the mill, and it could only be conjectured that in the place where it had been built the earth had opened up by divine power and swallowed it up and made it disappear from the eyes of men. The abbot then sent messengers to say to his brothers, "Rest from your labours now, for God has avenged the injury of our brethren."[5]

3. Having finished the course of his life, filled with such virtues, he passed to the Lord.[6] Afterwards at his tomb the possessed were cured and the blind recovered their sight. After his death those whom he had put at the head of the monasteries he had founded were established as abbots, with the consent of the bishops. Leobatius was established as abbot of Sennevières, in the diocese of Tours, where he lived in great sanctity and came to a great age. He died there and was buried there.

---

5. It no longer seems that James is right (loc.cit. in previous note) to argue that this practice of praying for three days for a specific purpose (as here and in *VP* IX) suggests a link with the early Irish church: the custom is too widespread in western monastic practice.

6. On July 28, presumably c.500.

XIX.   About the blessed Monegundis

The excellent gifts of divine favours which have been offered
from heaven to mankind cannot be conceived by the senses nor
expressed by words nor represented in writing, since the Saviour of the
world Himself, from the time of the creation, was seen by the
patriarchs, announced by the prophets, and in the end deigned to be
enclosed in the womb of Mary, ever virgin and ever pure, and the
omnipresent and immortal Creator suffered Himself to be clothed in
mortal flesh, to go to death for the redemption of men, who were dead
through sin, and to rise again victorious. Although we were gravely
wounded by the arrows of our sins and covered with wounds received
from brigands who had lain in wait, He mingled oil and wine, and led
us to the tavern of celestial medicine, that is to say, to the dogma of the
Holy Church. He exhorts us to live after the example of the saints and
to fortify ourselves by His incessant precepts. He gives us as models not
only men, but also the lesser sex, who fight not feebly, but with a virile
strength; He brings into His celestial kingdom not only men, who fight
as they should, but also women, who exert themselves in the struggle
with success. This we can see now in the blessed Monegundis, who left
her native land (just like that prudent queen who came to listen to the
wisdom of Solomon)[1] and came to the church of St Martin to admire
the miracles which took place there daily and to drink there as from a
priestly well, by which she was able to throw open the door to the
grove of Paradise.

1.   The most blessed Monegundis was from the city of
Chartres. She had been married according to her parents' wishes, and
had two daughters, which brought her a profound joy, so that she used
to say "God has made me fertile so that two daughters might be born
to me." But the bitterness of this world soon dissipated this earthly joy,
for both were brought to their death by a light fever. From that time the
mother was desolate; mourning and lamenting for the death of her
children she did not stop weeping, day and night, and neither her

---

1. The Queen of Sheba: see I Kings 10. Queen Ultrogotha, wife of Childebert I (511-558)
came to the church of St Martin "as if to hear the wisdom of Solomon": *VSM* I 12.

husband nor her friends nor any of her relations could console her. Finally she came to herself, and said, "If I do not receive any consolation for the death of my daughters I fear I may offend my Lord Jesus Christ. Thus forgetting these laments I shall sing with the blessed Job, consoling myself thus: The Lord gave, and the Lord taketh away; blessed be the name of the Lord (Job 1:21)." And saying that she took off her mourning clothes, and had a small room arranged for her, which only had one small window, by which she could see a little daylight. There, despising the vanities of the world and having nothing more to do with her husband, she devoted herself entirely to God, in whom she confided, praying for her sins and for the sins of the people. She had only one girl with her as her servant, to provide her with what was necessary. She took barley flour and ashes mixed with water, kneaded it all with care and made a dough from which she formed loaves with her own hands, and she baked them herself, and thus she comforted herself after long fasts. The rest of the food coming from her house she gave to the poor. It happened one day that the girl who used to serve her (I believe that she was seduced by the wiles of our enemy who always wishes to harm the good) withdrew from her service, saying "I cannot remain with a mistress who practises such abstinence; I prefer to go into the world, where I can eat and drink as much as I like." Five days passed after the departure of this girl, and her devout mistress had not taken her accustomed flour and water; she remained motionless, with Jesus Christ in her heart, in Whom the one who trusts cannot be overthrown, not by any whirlwind or storm. Nor did she think to sustain her life by any mortal food, but only by the word of God, as it is written,[2] recalling the proverb of the wisdom of Solomon, "The Lord will not suffer the soul of the righteous to famish" (Prov. 10:3), and again "The just shall live by faith" (Romans 1:17). But as the human body cannot survive without using earthly things, she asked by a humble prayer that He who produced manna from heaven for a people when it was hungry, and water from a rock when it was thirsty, might deign to give her the food necessary to sustain her weak body. Immediately, at her prayer, snow fell from the sky and covered the

---

2. Deuteronomy 8:3; Matthew 4:4.

ground.[3] She thanked God, and reached out of her window and collected some snow from the wall, and with this water she made bread as usual, which gave her food for another five days.

She had, next to her cell, a small garden in which she used to walk for exercise. She entered it one day, and walked around looking at the plants. A woman who had put wheat on the roof of her house in order to dry it, because it was a high place, began to watch the saint in an indiscreet way, filled with worldly thoughts. Soon her eyes darkened and she became blind. Recognising her fault she came to find the saint, and told her what had happened. She hastened to pray, and said, "Woe on me, if for a small offence done against my humble person, someone could have their eyes closed." And when she had finished her prayer she put her hand on this woman. As soon as she had made the sign of the cross the woman recovered her sight. A man from the same region, who had long since lost his hearing, came full of devotion to the cell of the saint, and his relations begged her to deign to put her hands on him. But she said that she was not worthy that Christ should deign to work such things through her; nevertheless she fell to the ground, as if she wished to kiss the traces of the feet of the Lord, and begged humbly for divine clemency for the man. While she was still lying on the ground the ears of the deaf man opened and he returned home joyfully, delivered from all sadness.

2.   Glorified among her relations because of such prodigies, Monegundis, in order to avoid the trap of vainglory, left her husband, her family, her whole house, and went, full of faith, to the basilica of the holy bishop Martin. While on her way she came to a village of the Touraine called Esvres, where relics of the blessed confessor Medard of Soissons were preserved;[4] that very night vigils were being celebrated.

---

3. Cf. the story of manna descending from heaven in Exodus 16.

4. *Evena*: cant. Montbazon, arr. Tours, dép. Indre-et-Loire. The basilica was built by St Perpetuus, bishop of Tours from 460 to 490: *LH* X 31(6). See V-T, no. 108. This church is still dedicated to St Medard. St Medard died a few years before Chlothar I (d.561), and Chlothar "had him buried with great pomp in the city of Soissons, and began to build over his remains the church which his son Sigibert later completed and embellished" (*LH* IV 19). It became the burial place of both Chlothar I and Sigibert, and hence one of the more important churches in the Frankish kingdom. This passage shows that the cult of the saint

The saint passed the night in attentive prayer, and then returned at the given time with the people to celebrate Mass. While the priests were in the midst of the service a young girl came up, swollen by the poison of a malignant pustule, and threw herself at her feet, saying, "Help me, for cruel death is going to snatch life from me." And she, prostrate in prayer in the usual fashion, prayed to God, the creator of all things, for this girl. Then she got up and made the sign of the cross. As a result the tumour opened, split into four, and the pus came out: the young girl was saved from importunate death. After that the blessed Monegundis arrived at the basilica of St Martin, and there, on her knees in front of the tomb, she gave thanks to God for being able to see the holy tomb with her own eyes. She settled herself in a small room to which she gave herself every day to prayer, fasts and vigils. And indeed this place was made glorious by her miracles. The daughter of a certain widow came there with her hands all contracted, and she was besought to pray and make the sign of salvation, and then she began to rub the fingers of the girl with her own hands, straightening out the fingers and tendons and finally freeing the palms and leaving her hands healthy. While these things were happening, her husband, having heard of the reputation of the saint, assembled his friends and neighbours and came after her and brought her back with him and put her in that same cell in which she had lived before. But she did not cease from the work she was used to, and she gave herself over to continual prayer and fasting, so that in the end she might reach the place where she wanted to be. Again she began the path which she desired, begging for the help of St Martin, that he who gave her the desire might give her the means. She came to the basilica and returned to the same cell she had inhabited before; she stayed there without any trouble, without being sought for again by her husband. She gathered together a small number of nuns in that place, and stayed there, persevering in faith and in prayer, eating only bread made of barley and not drinking any wine, except a little on feast-days, and then only diluted with much water. She did not have a soft bed of hay or fresh straw, but only one of interlaced twigs, which are

---

had spread within relatively few years of his death. See below n.8.

commonly called "mats";[5] she put this upon a bed-frame or on the ground, and it served her as a bench, a mattress, a pillow, a bed-spread, in a word all that she needed for a bed. She taught those whom she had brought to live with her how to make these mats. And living there, praising God, she gave to many sick people, after she had prayed, healing cures.

3. A certain woman presented to her her daughter, who was covered with open sores and, as some say, had for this reason become a prostitute. She prayed, took some saliva and anointed the open wounds and made the young girl healthy with the same power which He had used when with saliva He formed the eyes of a man blind from birth. A young boy, an inhabitant of the place, had drunk a noxious substance in a drink, in consequence of which, it was said, serpents had been born inside his body, causing him great pain by their biting, so that he could not enjoy even one moment of rest. He could neither drink nor eat, and if eventually he took something he brought it all up again. He was brought to the blessed woman, and he begged her to cleanse him by her power. And although she protested that she was unworthy to accomplish such a miracle, she nevertheless gave in to the prayers of the young man's parents, and feeling his stomach and stroking it gently with her hand she felt the place where the corruption of poisonous snakes was hidden. She took then the green leaf of a vine, moistened it with saliva, made the sign of the cross on it, and put it on the stomach of the boy. The pain was a little eased, and he slept on a bed, he who formerly had been deprived of sleep because of his continuous pain. After an hour, he got up to purge his stomach, poured out the germ of the poisonous race, and returned cured, giving thanks to the handmaid of God.[6] Another young boy was paralysed, and was brought in the arms of others to the blessed woman, and begged her to cure him. She lay down in prayer and poured out a prayer to the Lord for him. Her prayer done, she took the child by the hand, put him on his feet, and sent him away

---

5. *quas vulgo mattas vocant.* The word seems often used in a monastic context: cf the Rule of St Benedict, 55.13, "for bedding the monks will need a mat (*matta*), a woollen blanket and a light covering as well as a pillow", transl. in *RB 1980: the Rule of St Benedict*, ed. T. Fry (Collegeville, Minnesota, 1981), p. 263.

6. This miracle is mentioned also at *GC* 24.

cured. A blind woman who was brought there begged her to place her hands on her, but she replied, "What is it between you and me, men of God? Does not St Martin live here, who each day shines with the work of his miracles? Go to him and pray that he may deign to visit you. For I am only a sinner; what can I do?" But the woman persisted in her request, saying "God daily accomplishes remarkable deeds through those who fear His name. That is why I came to you as a suppliant, since you have received the grace of healing from God." And the servant of God, greatly moved, placed her hands on the buried eyes, and immediately the cataracts disappeared, and the woman who had been blind could see the world spread out in front of her. Many possessed people also came to her. As soon as she put her hands on them she put the wicked enemy to flight and brought back health; and of all those to whom the holy woman allowed access, none had to wait long for a cure.

4. But already the time was approaching when God would call her to Him, and her strength began to desert her. Seeing this, the nuns who were with her wept bitterly and said "And to whom do you leave us, holy mother?[7] To whom do you entrust your daughters whom you have assembled here to look on God?" She told them, weeping, "If you keep peace and holiness, God will protect you, and you will have the great bishop St Martin as shepherd. And I shall not be far from you, for if you invoke me I shall be in your hearts." But the nuns implored her, saying "Many sick people will come to us, asking to receive your blessing, and what shall we do when they see that you are no more? We shall be confused, and send them away, since we shall no longer contemplate your face. We beg you, then, since you are going from our eyes, that you deign at least to bless some oil and salt that we can give to the sick who ask for a blessing." And she blessed some oil and salt for them, which they preserved with great care. And thus the blessed woman died in peace;[8] she was buried in her cell,[9] and she manifested

---

7. Cf. *GC* 104 on death of St Radegund, and see above XV n.7.

8. Her feast-day is July 2. She is not mentioned in *LH*. She clearly died some time after St Medard of Soissons, because she visited his relics at Evena (*VP* XIX 2): he probably died about 557/8 (see above n.4).

herself thereafter by many miracles, for many sick people were cured, after her death, by the blessing which we have just mentioned.[10] A deacon called Boso had a foot which was very swollen because of a malignant pustule, so that he could no longer walk. He had himself carried to the tomb of the holy woman and said a prayer there. The sisters then took some of the oil that the saint had left and put it on his foot. Immediately the pustule opened, the venom flowed out and the man was cured. A blind man led to the same tomb began to pray, and was overcome by sleep; he slept and saw in a dream the blessed woman, who said to him, "I judge myself unworthy of being ranked with the saints; nevertheless you will recover here the sight of one eye. Go then to the feet of the blessed Martin and prostrate yourself in front of him in the compunction of your soul. He will give you back the use of your other eye." This man woke up and, having recovered the sight of one eye, he went where he was told, and there he begged for the power of the blessed confessor; the night was expelled from the blind eye, and he left with his full sight. A dumb person also came to fall at the tomb of the holy woman, and his heart was so contrite with faith that he moistened the floor of the cell with floods of tears; when he stood up he found his tongue loosened by divine power, and he left. Another dumb person came then, and beginning to pray he implored for the help of the blessed woman with his heart, not being able to do so with his mouth. A little of the blessed oil and salt was put in his mouth, and immediately there escaped from his lips blood mixed with pus, and he obtained the use of his voice. A man who had fever approached this tomb also, and he had hardly touched the cloth which covered it when the fever calmed, and he was cured. A cripple called Marcus was carried to the tomb of the blessed woman and prayed there for a long time. At the ninth hour he stood up on his own feet and walked home. A boy called Leodinus who had been gravely ill for four months and could not walk or even eat, because of the violence of a persistent fever, was brought to the tomb almost dead; he found health there, and arose

---

9. Her cell was near St Martin's tomb. Her small monastery is mentioned in a charter of 1031, but disappears after that. The relics were later placed in St-Pierre-le-Puellier. See V-T no. 325.

10. In *GC* 24 Gregory says that he will not report these miracles, since he has related many in the book he has written of her life: this refers to *VP* XIX.

from the tomb restored to life. What should I say of all the others who have been cured of fever, just by kissing the cloth on the tomb, with faith? What should I say of the possessed who are led to the cell of the blessed woman, and who, when they cross the sacred threshold, recover their senses? The demon did not delay to leave their body when it felt the power of this saint working through Our Lord Jesus Christ, who freely gives eternal reward to those who fear His name.

XX.   About Leobardus, a recluse

The Church of the faithful is being built every time the acts of the saints are reported with devotion. And although the greatest joy is felt with those who have led a religious life from their childhood and deserve to arrive happily at the port of perfection, one should also rejoice, as God ordains, in those who turn from the world and have had the strength to complete the pious enterprise with the help of divine mercy.

1. The blessed Leobardus was born in the Auvergne and was in truth not of senatorial family, although he was of free birth.[1] He had God in his heart from his childhood, and if he did not excel in birth he did outshine others by his glorious merits. When it was time he was sent with the other children to school, where he learnt some of the psalms by heart, and without knowing that he would one day be a cleric he unknowingly prepared himself for the Lord's service. When he had arrived at the age of legal majority his parents, following the custom of the world, wanted him to give to a young girl a pledge that he would take her as his wife. When he showed himself unwilling to do this his father said, "My dear son, why do you resist your father's will and do not marry, so that your seed can preserve our family for future generations? For we are just working in vain if no-one comes after us to profit from it. Why fill our house with riches, if nobody from our family will use them? Why should we spend money buying so many slaves for our estates, if all of them are going to pass into the possession of a stranger? The Holy Scriptures attest that children must obey the voice of their parents,[2] and beware if you show yourself disobedient towards your parents, lest you find yourself punished by heaven!" He spoke thus, although there was in fact another son, thinking that since the boy was so young he would easily be able to get him to do what he wanted. Leobardus in the end gave a ring to his betrothed, offered her a kiss, bestowed shoes on her, and celebrated a feast on the

---

1. Cf. what Gregory says of Patroclus, *VP* IX 1.

2. Ephesians 6:1.

day of his betrothal.[3] After this his father and mother left this world, overtaken by the sleep of death, after having completed the course of their life. When Leobardus and his brother had finished the time of mourning, the former went to his brother's house, laden with wedding presents, and found him so drunk that he did not recognise Leobardus or let him into the house. Leobardus sighed and wept, and went away. He came to a barn filled with hay, and after tying up his horse and feeding it, he lay down on the hay to sleep. In the midst of the night he woke, got up from his bed, and, stretching out his hands to heaven, gave thanks to Almighty God that he was, that he lived, and that God nourished him with his gifts, and he continued thus for a long time. He uttered long sighs, and abundant tears ran down his cheeks, and Almighty God, who foreknows and predestines men to be conform-ed to the image of His Son,[4] touched his heart and inspired him to leave the world in order to serve the worship of God.

2. Then, as if now the priest of his own soul, he began to preach to himself, saying, "What are you doing, my soul? Why do you still hesitate? The world is vain, its lusts are vain, its glory is vain, everything that is in it is vanity.[5] It is better to leave it and to follow God than to compromise with its works." Having thus spoken, when the light of day began to bring light back to the world he got on his horse and started to go home. As he went cheerfully on his way he began to ponder what he should do and where he should go. And he said, "I shall go to the tomb of the blessed Martin, from which proceeds a healing power. For I believe that his prayer will open a way for me to go to God, since his prayer to the Lord has brought the dead back from Hell." And he continued on his way, always praying, and entered the basilica of St Martin, near which he remained for several days. Then he crossed the river and came with devotion to a cell near Marmoutier[6] in which once a certain Alaric had lived. There he began to make parchment with his own hands, and prepared it for writing; there he learnt to understand

---

3. Cf. *VP* XVI 1.

4. Quoting Romans 8:29.

5. Cf. Ecclesiastes 1:2.

6. *Maius monasterium*: founded by St Martin just across the river Loire from Tours.

the Holy Scriptures and to memorise the Psalms of David, which had long passed from his mind. Instructed in this way by the reading of the Bible, he recognised the truth of what the Lord had formerly inspired in his heart. And do not think that these things which I relate are mere fictions; as God is my witness, I had them from the mouth of the blessed Leobardus himself. After a short time he was so perfectly humble that he was honoured by all. And he took a pick and dug out the stone of his cell in order to make it larger. In this cell he gave himself up with delight to fasting, praying, singing psalms and reading, and he never ceased in the celebration of divine worship and in prayer; from time to time he used to write, to distract himself from wicked thoughts.

3. Meanwhile, in order to show himself always as the enemy of the servants of God, the Tempter took advantage of a quarrel which had arisen between the saint and his neighbours over monastic matters and gave him the idea of leaving his cell and going to another. When we were in that place, coming there to pray as usual, he showed us the corruption of the poison which ravaged his heart. I sighed deeply with great sadness, and began to exhort him and assure him that it was an artifice of the devil. And when I had left him I sent him books of the *Life of the Fathers* and the *Institution of the Monks*,[7] in order that he might learn what hermits had to do and with what care monks had to live. He read them, and not only did he banish from his mind the evil thought that he had had, but also developed his learning so much that he astonished us by his facility in speaking of such matters. He expressed himself in such a gentle manner, and his exhortations were full of charm; he had solicitude for the poor, reproof for kings and assiduous prayer for all God-fearing clerics. He was not like those who

---

7. Rufinus' *Vitae Patrum* and John Cassian's 12 books *De Institutis Coenobiorum*: these were the two books St Romanus obtained from Abbot Sabinus at the outset of his monastic career: see *VPJ* I 3 (Martine pp. 252-3). On Cassian's monastic ideas, see P. Rousseau, *Ascetics, Authority and the Church in the Age of Jerome and Cassian* (Oxford, 1978).

delight in wearing long hair and long beards,[8] for at fixed times he used to cut his hair and beard. He remained twenty-two years occupied in this manner in his cell, and obtained so much grace from God that with his saliva alone he could banish the poison from malignant pustules. He quenched the fire of fevers with wine which he had sanctified by the sign of the cross. He deserved the power to repress the heat of fever in others, he who extinguished the heat of wicked passions in himself. One day a blind man came to him who wept with humility over his misfortune, and begged the saint to touch his blind eyes with his hand. He refused for a long time; but finally, conquered by the tears of this man and touched by compassion, he prayed to the Lord for three days, and on the fourth he put his hands on the man's eyes and said, "Almighty God, Only Son of God the Father, who reigns with Him and the Holy Spirit, world without end, Who gave light to one born blind with the saliva of Your blessed mouth, give sight to this man, Your servant, so that he may recognise that You are the Almighty Lord." And saying that he traced the sign of the cross on the eyes of the blind man, and immediately the shadows dissipated and sight was restored to him. Abbot Eustachius, who was present, can attest the truth of this miracle.

4. In the end, broken by the continual labour of cutting into the rock (since he continued to excavate into the hillside), worn out by the austerity of his fasts, although strengthened by his incessant prayers, he began to feel himself become weaker, little by little. One day when he was particularly tired he called us to him. We went, and after having wept for the necessity of his death he begged us, a sinner, to give him communion. He received it, and drank the wine, and said, "My time is finished. God ordains that I shall be delivered from the bonds of this body, but it will take some days. I shall be called by Him before the holy day of Easter." O happy man, who served the Creator of all things so faithfully that he knew by divine revelation the moment of his death! It was the tenth month of the year when he said these things, and in the

---

8. Like, as Krusch notes, St Martin himself, whose scruffy appearance was detested by his more worldly episcopal colleagues: Sulpicius, *Life of St Martin*, 9: transl., e.g., by F.R. Hoare, *The Western Fathers* (London, 1954).

twelfth he fell ill again.[9] One Sunday he called his servant to him and said, "Prepare me some food to take, for I am very weak." And he replied, "I shall do it, master." And he said, "Go, and see if the office is finished and if the people are leaving Mass." He said that not because he wished to take food but so that nobody might witness his death. The servant returned, and when he entered the cell he found the man of God, his body stretched out, his eyes closed, and his spirit departed.[10] Which proves clearly that the angels took him, since the holy hero wished nobody to be present at his death. At the sight the man who had served him cried out and wept. The other brothers ran up. The body was washed, and dressed in a suitable way, and he was put into a tomb which he himself had cut out of the rock in his cell. No faithful person will doubt that he is in the company of the saints.

---

9. The tenth month for Gregory was December; the twelfth was February. The year began in March.

10. His feast-day is January 18: perhaps this was the date of the translation of his relics, rather than his death, which Gregory seems to say happened in February. The year is not known, but it must be after Gregory came as bishop to Tours in 573, and since he had remained there for 22 years (some of that presumably before Gregory's gift of books) it is likely that he died quite late in Gregory's episcopate.

ABBREVIATIONS

BAR   British Archaeological Reports

GC   Liber in Gloria Confessorum

GM   Liber in Gloria Martyrum

LH   Decem Libri Historiarum

MGH   Monumenta Germaniae Historica

PLRE   The Prosopography of the Later Roman Empire

SSRM   Scriptores Rerum Merovingicarum

VP   Liber Vitae Patrum

VPJ   Vita Patrum Iurensium

VSJ   Liber de Passione et Virtutibus Sancti Iuliani Martyris

VSM   Libri de Virtutibus Sancti Martini Episcopi

V-T   Vieillard-Troiekouroff, 1976

BIBLIOGRAPHY

Main Editions of *VP*

Badius, I., *Beati Gregorii Turonensis episcopi Historiarum praecipue Gallicarum libri X. In Vitas Patrum fere sui temporis lib. I* etc. (In aedibus Ascensianis, 1512).

Ruinart, Dom T., *Sancti Georgii Florentii Gregorii episcopi Turonensis opera omnia* etc (Paris, 1679).

Migne, J.-P., *Patrologia Latina*, 71 (Paris, 1846) [essentially a reprint of Ruinart].

Krusch, B., *Gregorii Episcopi Turonensis Miracula et Opera Minora*, MGH SSRM I (1885), pp. 661-744; reprinted as a separate volume in 1969, MGH SSRM I part II, pp. 211-294.

Translations of *VP*

Marolles, M. de, *L'Histoire des François de S. Grégoire, II. volume. La seconde partie des Histoires de S. Grégoire, evesque de Tours, contenant ses livres de la Gloire des Martyres et des Confesseurs, avec les quatre livres de la Vie de S. Martin et celui de la Vie des Pères* (Paris, 1668) [French]

Bordier, H.L., *Les Livres des Miracles et autres opuscules de Georges Florent Grégoire évêque de Tours revus et collationnés sur de nouveaux manuscrits et traduits pour la Société de l'Histoire de France* (Paris, 1857-64) [French]

Peters, E., ed., *Monks, Bishops and Pagans: Christian Culture in Gaul and Italy, 500-700* (Philadelphia, 1975) [translations by W.C. McDermott of Gregory's prefaces, *VSM* I, *VP* VI and VII, "The Seven Sleepers of Ephesus" and "The Seven Wonders of the World"]

Select Secondary Works

Aigrain, R., 1953. *L'Hagiographie, ses Sources, ses Méthodes, son Histoire* (Paris).

Auerbach, E., 1953. *Mimesis: the Representation of Reality in Western Literature* (Princeton) [pp. 77-99 on Gregory].

Auerbach, E., 1965. *Literary Language and its Public in Late Antiquity and in the Middle Ages* (London).

Beck, H.G.J., 1950. *The Pastoral Care of Souls in South-East France during the Sixth Century* (Rome).

Bratton, T.L., 1979. *Tours: from Roman "Civitas" to Merovingian Episcopal Center, c.275-650 AD.* (Ph.D. dissertation. Bryn Mawr).

Brennan, B., 1985. "The conversion of the Jews of Clermont in AD 576", *Journal of Theological Studies* 36.

Brown, P., 1977. *Relics and Social Status in the Age of Gregory of Tours* (Stenton lecture, 1976: Reading), reprinted in Brown 1982, pp. 222-50.

Brown, P., 1981. *The Cult of the Saints* (Chicago/London).

Brown, P., 1982. *Society and the Holy in Late Antiquity* (London).

Buchner, R., 1955. *Gregor von Tours: Zehn Bücher Geschichten* (Darmstadt).

Clarke, H.B. and Brennan, M., eds., 1981. *Columbanus and Merovingian Monasticism* (BAR Int. Ser. 113, Oxford).

Collins, R., 1983. "Theodebert I, 'Rex Magnus Francorum'", in Wormald 1983, pp. 7-33.

Corbett, J.H., 1981. "The Saint as Patron in the Work of Gregory of Tours", *Journal of Medieval History* 7, pp. 1-13.

De Clercq, C., 1963. *Concilia Galliae, A.511-A.695* (Corpus Christianorum, Ser. Lat. 148A, Turnhout).

De Nie, G., 1979. "Roses in January: a Neglected Dimension in Gregory of Tours' *Historiae*", *Journal of Medieval History* 5, pp. 259-89.

De Nie, G., 1985. "The spring, the seed and the tree: Gregory of Tours on the wonders of nature", *Journal of Medieval History* 11, pp. 89-135.

De Nie, G. 1987 *Views from a Many-Windowed Tower: Studies of Imagination in the Works of Gregory of Tours* (Amsterdam)

Flint, V.I.J., 1991. *The Rise of Magic in Early Medieval Europe* (Princeton/Oxford)

Fournier, G., 1962. *Le Peuplement rural en Basse-Auvergne dans le Haut Moyen Age* (Paris).

Goffart, W., 1980. *Barbarians and Romans, A.D. 418-584. The Techniques of Accommodation* (Princeton).

Goffart, W., 1985. "The conversions of Bishop Avitus and similar passages in Gregory of Tours", in J. Neusner and E.R. Frerichs, ed., *To See Ourselves as Others See Us: Christians, Jews, "Others" in Late Antiquity* (Chico, CA), 473-497; repr. in Goffart 1989, pp. 293-317.

Goffart, W., 1988. *The Narrators of Barbarian History: Jordanes, Gregory of Tours, Bede and Paul the Deacon* (Princeton)

Goffart, W., 1989. *Rome's Fall and After* (London)

Heinzelmann, M., 1982. "Gallische Prosopographie, 260-527", *Francia* 10, pp. 531-718.

Hillgarth, J.N., 1969. *The Conversion of Western Europe, 350-750* (Engelwood Cliffs, New Jersey).

James, E., 1977. *The Merovingian Archaeology of South-West Gaul*, 2 vols. (BAR Supplem. Series 25, Oxford).

James, E., 1981. "Archaeology and the Merovingian monastery", in Clarke and Brennan, pp. 33-55.

James, E., 1982. *The Origins of France: from Clovis to the Capetians, 500-1000* (London).

James, E., 1983. "Beati pacifici: Bishops and the Law in Sixth-Century Gaul", in J.A. Bossy, ed., *Disputes and Settlements: Law and Human Relations in the West* (Cambridge), pp. 25-46.

James, E., 1984. "Bede and the tonsure question", *Peritia* 3, 85-98.

James, E., 1988. *The Franks* (Oxford)

Jones, A.H.M., 1964. *The Later Roman Empire, 284-602*, 3 vols. (Oxford).

Jones, C.W., 1947. *Saints' Lives and Chronicles in Early England* (Ithaca, N.Y.)

McCready, W.D., 1989. *Signs of Sanctity. Miracles in the Thought of Gregory the Great* (Toronto)

Martine, F., 1968. *Vie des Pères du Jura* (Sources Chrétiennes 142, Paris).

Mathisen, R.W., 1984. "The family of Georgius Florentius Gregorius and the bishops of Tours", *Medievalia et Humanistica* 12, pp. 83-95.

Niermeyer, J.F., 1976. *Mediae Latinitatis Lexicon Minus* (Leiden).

Piétri, L., 1983. *La ville de Tours du IVe au VIe siècle: Naissance d'une ville chrétienne* (Rome)

Prosopography of the Later Roman Empire, The: vol. 1 (A.D. 260-395), ed. A.H.M. Jones et al. (Cambridge, 1971); vol. 2 (A.D. 395-527), ed. J.R. Martindale (Cambridge, 1980).

Rouche, M., 1979. *L'Aquitaine des Wisigoths aux Arabes, 418-781: Naissance d'une Région* (Paris).

Scheibelreiter, G., 1983. *Der Bischof in merowingischer Zeit* (Vienna)

Selle-Hosbach, K., 1974. *Prosopographie Merowingischer Amtsträger in der Zeit von 511 bis 613* (Bonn).

Stancliffe, C., 1983. *St. Martin and his Hagiographer: History and Miracle in Sulpicius Severus* (Oxford).

Thorpe, L., 1974. *Gregory of Tours: History of the Franks* (Harmondsworth).

Van Dam, R., 1985. *Leadership and Community in Late Antique Gaul* (Berkeley).

Van Dam, R., 1988. *Gregory of Tours: Glory of the Martyrs* (Liverpool).

Van Dam, R., 1988. *Gregory of Tours: Glory of the Confessors* (Liverpool).

Vieillard-Troiekouroff, M., 1976. *Les Monuments Religieux de la Gaule d'après les Oeuvres de Grégoire de Tours* (Paris).

Wallace-Hadrill, J.M., 1951. "The Work of Gregory of Tours in the Light of Historical Research", *Transactions of the Royal Historical Society* 5th ser. 1, reprinted in Wallace-Hadrill 1962, pp. 49-70.

Wallace Hadrill, J.M., 1962. *The Long-Haired Kings and other studies in Frankish history* (London).

Wallace-Hadrill, J.M., 1983. *The Frankish Church* (Oxford).

Weidemann, M., 1982. *Kulturgeschichte der Merowingerzeit nach den Werken Gregors von Tours* (two vols.) (Mainz).

Wood, I.N., 1977. "Kings, Kingdoms and Consent", in P.H. Sawyer and I.N. Wood, eds., *Early Medieval Kingship* (Leeds), pp. 6-29.

Wood, I.N., 1979. "Early Merovingian devotion in town and country", D. Baker, ed., *Studies in Church History* 16, pp. 61-76.

Wood, I.N., 1981. "A prelude to Columbanus: the monastic achievement in the Burgundian territories", in Clarke and Brennan, pp. 3-32.

Wood, I.N., 1983. "The Ecclesiastical Politics of Merovingian Clermont", in Wormald 1983, pp. 34-57.

Wormald, P. et al., ed., 1983. *Ideal and Reality in Frankish and Anglo-Saxon Society. Studies presented to J.M. Wallace-Hadrill* (Oxford).

Zöllner, E., 1970. *Geschichte der Franken, bis zur Mitte des 6. Jahrhunderts* (Munich).

INDEX OF PEOPLE AND PLACES

(The index relates only to the translation, and excludes Biblical names.)